THE BUNGALOW AND THE TENT OR A VISIT TO CEYLON

THE BUNGALOW AND THE TENT OR A VISIT TO CEYLON

EDWARD SULLIVAN

GYAN

Published by

GYAN

Gyan Publishing House
5, Ansari Road
Daryaganj, New Delhi-110002
Phone: 011-47034999, 9811692060
E-mail: books@gyanbooks.com

Distribution Network
gyanbooks.com
India, USA, Canada, UK, Australia, France

© Publisher
All rights reserved. No part of this work may be reproduced, stored, adapted, or transmitted in any form or by any means, electronic, mechanical, photocopying, micro-filming, recording or otherwise, or translated in any language, without the prior written permission of the copyright owner and the publisher.

ISBN : 978-81-212-3187-9 (PB)
First Published, 1854

2nd Impression 2020

Printed at: Gyan Press, Delhi.

The book is sold subject to the condition that it shall not, by way of trade or otherwise, be lent, resold, hired out, or otherwise circulated without the prior publisher's written consent.

The Bungalow and the Tent or a Visit to Ceylon
Author: Edward Sullivan

DEDICATED

TO LADY SULLIVAN

BY

HER AFFECTIONATE SON.

PREFACE.

BACON announced some centuries ago, that Nature had ceased to dispense novelties. "Nothing new can be either found or done, read or related: nothing new but as the moon is new, the old moon with her face turned the other way." Time has endorsed this observation, and the truth of the venerable saw touching the superiority of "old books, old wine, old friends, and old ——," (I forget the fourth, but don't think it is "old women,") becomes daily more patent. The following pages consequently cannot be expected to contain anything new, otherwise than as an old picture in a fresh light is new.

Coffee-planting and Buddhism, elephant-shooting and leeches, are probably as familiar to many as cricket or crotchet.

"Friend, be not tedious," said the Rajah of Travancore to a Christian missionary, in the sixteenth century, "remember life is short." I have endeavoured to pay due attention to this admirable advice; and if what I have written be wearisome, the offence can scarcely be visited on the quantity.

It has been laid to the charge of many authors, "that they deprive themselves of sleep, in order to procure it for their readers." I plead a conscientious "not guilty" to this allegation. "Blessed be the man who invented sleep," says the immortal Squire; and blessed be he, I repeat, who imparts it by any means, whether Doctor, Preacher, Author, or Bore.

LONDON,
Oct. 15, 1854.

CONTENTS.

PAGE

CHAPTER VII.

CHAPTER VIII.

CHAPTER IX.

CHAPTER X.

CHAPTER XI.

CHAPTER XII.

CHAPTER XIII.

CHAPTER XIV.

CHAPTER XV.

THE

BUNGALOW AND THE TENT.

CHAPTER I.

OVERLAND ROUTE—POINT DE GALLE—EARLY NAVIGATORS—CINGALESE COSTUME—"TERTIUM QUIDS"—JEWELS.

I KNOW of no spot in either hemisphere, where tropical nature indulges in more marvellous redundancy than at Point de Galle; and after the sun-dried regions successively brought under the notice of the overland traveller, this luxuriance becomes still more remarkable. Malta is less vegetable than Gibraltar, Suez more sapless than either; and, excepting the Oasis of Cairo, and a distant view of the serpentine valley of the Nile, there is actually not a green spot from the Needles to the Strait of Babelmandel. When, after ten dreary, stifling days in the Red Sea, the passenger is landed at that culminating point of desolation (in this planet, at least), the Crater of Aden, the bias of his mind, as regards the gorgeous East, will have been disturbed, the current of his imagination dried up, and he will probably return to his steamer with the disagreeable conviction that he is the victim of misplaced confidence, that tropical luxuriance is a humbug, and that he and his companions are the only green things he is likely to see, until he finds his way back to less husky and more aqueous climes. I don't suppose any two places on the globe's surface illustrate more strongly than Aden and Point de Galle, the partiality with which nature has distributed her blessings. One might imagine the former to have been totally overlooked when vegetation was being served out; while it seems as though Pan, Pales, Flora, or Pomona, or whoever was entrusted with that duty, had, in a frolicsome spirit of exuberant generosity, emptied the cornucopia of vegetation intended for a whole continent, on the summit of the latter. It is literally smothered in verdant luxuriance, which heaped, massed, jumbled together in indescribable profusion, is barely restrained within its natural limits by the envious waves of the opposing ocean. At the entrance of the harbour are three or four detached rocks, on which some cocoa palms have established themselves, and there, without any nourishment, apparently, but the salt brine, they flourish and bear fruit, and remind the scholar of the Isolated Rock of Charybdis, on whose "crown," as Palinurus in blank verse poetically informed Æneas,

> "A fig's green branches rise
> And shoot a lofty forest to the skies."

The harbour at Point de Galle is small, and not too secure, and the entrance narrow and intricate. Plans *ad nauseam* for improving it have been proposed, discussed, and deferred, but nothing has as yet been done. The subject, formerly one of almost local interest, is now of considerable public importance. Galle is a harbour of great and increasing resort: no less than a dozen steamers coal there regularly every month, besides numerous stray visitors.

The more one reads of the early maritime discoveries in both hemispheres, the more astonished one becomes at the almost invariable good fortune that attended the first navigators, and enabled them successfully to brave shoals and currents, monsoons and hurricanes, which even in these days of screws and paddle-wheels, are encircled by dangers and difficulties of no slight nature. Within the incredibly short space of twenty years from the landing of Vasco de Gama on the west coast of India, Almeida, Perez, Castro, Albuquerque, and others, explored the coasts of Java, Malacca, Ceylon, India, and Siam, making settlements and founding factories in all these countries; and it was not until they attempted to penetrate into the Celestial empire, that they came to a land where they were not only unwelcome, but where the men with "long beards and large eyes were viewed in the light of enemies. The exploits of the Portuguese adventurers of the sixteenth century in the eastern hemisphere lose nothing by comparison with those of their rivals, the Spaniards, in the west. Lorenzo d'Almeida, a companion of Camoëns and Vasco de Gama, one of that gallant band I have mentioned, who, in the beginning of the sixteenth century, succeeded, by their energy and self-devotion, in creating a golden age, though a transient one, for Portugal, stumbled upon Point de Galle, in his voyage from Calicut to the Laccadives, or Hundred Thousand Isles, and by that accident brought to the world's notice a most fertile island, and cast amongst scholars and antiquarians an apple of discord, that has proved a most fruitful source of discussion and debate.

However interesting it may be to such literati to determine whether Ceylon is actually the land of Dedan alluded to by the Prophets, or whether it is the island of Taprobăne, mentioned by Ovid,* to the passing traveller it is probably a

* Ex. Pont. 8—Ec. 5. v. 80.

matter of considerable indifference. He cannot help remarking, however, that the words both of Ezekiel, ("Men of Dedan were thy merchants; many isles were the merchandise of thine hand: they brought thee for a present horns of ivory and ebony;" chap. xxvii. 15,) and of Jeremiah, ("Flee ye, turn back, dwell deep, O inhabitants of Dedan;" chap. xlix. 9,) imply an amount of nautical proficiency in the inhabitants of that day, which to those of the present is totally wanting.

The Cingalese of the 19th century A.D. are no sailors, whatever they may have been in the 9th century B.C.; and if they had now to undertake a voyage to the Red Sea, I imagine they would find considerable difficulty in effecting any insurance under 100 per cent.

With the exception of the old Dutch fort, (which answers very well the purpose for which such buildings seem to serve in the colonies, namely, that of keeping her Majesty's troops and the civil employés some fifteen degrees hotter than they would otherwise be,) I fancy the Bay presents very much the same appearance now as it did in those distant ages to which I have alluded.

The "forest primeval" still contends with the ocean for the possession of the sandy shore, and canoes, almost as primeval, with outriggers and sails of the simplest nature, and paddlers in the most primitive buff, still stud and labour across the bay, fishing or boarding vessels, much as they might have done some 3,000 years ago. In the place, however, of boarding Tyrian galleys with "benches of Cypress inlaid with ivory, with fine linen of Egypt adorned with embroidery for sails," and making hard bargains with keen old Tyrians, they find themselves on board the more useful but scarcely picturesque vessels of the Peninsular and Oriental Company, and dispose of their glass emeralds and Birmingham snuff-boxes to verdant griffs, who purchase with great enthusiasm at something over 500 per cent. of their real value.

On landing, which you do possibly with considerable uneasiness in one of the afore-mentioned canoes, you are beset by a nondescript and anomalous crowd, attired in scanty petticoats, reaching to the ankles, parasols in their hands, and their long hair drawn off the forehead, and turned up behind with a high tortoiseshell comb. These peculiarities of dress, together with their full busts and effeminate features, and the waddling gait caused by the restraint of the petticoats, impress the traveller with the idea that he has landed amongst a nation of women; but when assured of their masculine gender, the similarity amongst them all is so great that he immediately jumps to the conclusion that, on the other hand, there are no women at all; and it is not till he has had some days' experience that he begins with any success to discriminate between the male and female portion of the community. The only visible distinction between the sexes consists in the women wearing rather shorter jackets than the men, enjoying generally rather coarser features, and dispensing with the masculine appendages of combs and parasols.

The Cingalese are, without exception, the most unnaturally effeminate race in appearance that I have ever seen; and even after several months' residence in the island, one is continually confounded and disgusted by the appearance of creatures from the age of ten to fifteen, whom, but for the certain knowledge that they were men, one would certainly conclude to be women. From the time of the Lady Grenadier in Charles XII.'s army, who, adorned with a beard a yard and a half long, was taken prisoner at the battle of Pultowa, down to the Spanish Whiskeranda of last year, instances of bearded women of a masculine presence have been numerous. And indeed in the chivalric days of old, in time of war, the ladies, both amongst the Athenians and the Lombards, not unfrequently tried to change their feminine into a martial appearance, by arranging the hair of the head under the chin to represent a beard,—but this was only on occasions, and for a purpose; but for a whole nation of men to assimilate to what one has always considered the peculiar fashions of women, is disgusting in the extreme. This total absence of the strong line of demarcation, that in all other countries marks the individuality of the sexes, is so unnatural, that one receives an impression of unconquerable contempt and dislike for the entire race so mingled, and this feeling is never shaken off. So dearly do the Cingalese prize the fashion of wearing high combs, that the tyranny of the Tamul kings could devise no more galling and offensive enaction against the liberty and predilections of their low country subjects, than by forbidding the use of that article. It is remarkable that Julius Cæsar attacked the forefathers of our Gallic neighbours on the same tender point, and obliged them to doff their *chevelure* as a token of submission.

I have always considered that the trade of the hair merchants in France, who attend fairs for the purpose of persuading the peasant girls to dispose of their locks for a few paltry livres, is so unnatural and so cruel that, like the slave trade, it ought to be repressed *vi et armis*, but if these said merchants could visit Ceylon, and, either by persuasion or force, deprive these long-haired nondescripts of their topknots, it would, on the other hand, be a benefit to society in general, and to those opposed to hyacinthine curls for the genus *homo* in particular. When watching those mincing conceited creatures sitting in groups, combing and anointing their long back hair, I have felt infinitely more disgust at their occupation, than I ever experienced in viewing the amicable phrenological investigations mutually exchanged by Italian beggars at Naples and elsewhere; and I have often longed, like "Katharina," to perform "with a three-legged stool" the same operation on their noddles, that they were performing with the genuine shell.

Most strangers have heard of the number and the varieties of precious stones in the Island of Ceylon, but the reality, as presented to them at Galle, must far exceed their most sanguine expectations. Plates of emeralds, rubies, sapphires, topaz, cats' eyes, &c. &c., are offered for sale in a profusion and of a size that remind one of those plucked by Aladdin in the enchanted garden. The seediest of Mussulman and Cingalese hawkers produce from the filthiest of turbans and petticoats the most resplendent of jewels. The unwary traveller, although attracted and admiring, probably begins by being very wary and cautious, and *pooh poohs* every stone, good, bad, or indifferent, as glass; but he gradually yields to the positive assurances of the dealers, and to the dazzling nature of their wares, and generally concludes by giving five or six guineas for stones which he fondly believes are worth twenty or thirty times that sum. This agreeable illusion lasts till, displaying his purchase with triumph to some more experienced hand, he is coolly told they are glass, and consoled by the assurance that they are very good imitations, and might have deceived a far better judge.

Precious stones are actually found in considerable numbers and of great beauty in Ceylon (indeed, that island and Burmah supply the greatest number of jewels for the markets), but all of any purity and value are immediately purchased by the agents for the London and Paris markets, and only the very inferior ones find their way into the hands of the hawkers. Those purchased by the griffs and greenhorns, are almost invariably good Birmingham glass, the manufacture of which is now so perfect, and the imitation so superior in appearance to the genuine article, that an artful vendor has no difficulty in disposing of the glass, even in preference to the jewel. A fellow-passenger of mine gave 24*l.* for four emerald rings, that afterwards proved to be every one of them glass, and worth some 24 pence.

CHAPTER II.

METHOD OF DRIVING—GALLE TO COLOMBO—COCOA-NUT GROVES—CASSIA AND CINNAMON—COLOMBO—CLIMATE.

THE hotels at Galle are of course bad, as at what place peopled by English are they not? So, after admiring for a couple of days the wild, almost rank luxuriance of the environs, we proceeded to Colombo.

Travelling, doubtless, disabuses one of certain vulgar, narrow-minded prejudices concerning the invariable use for which certain objects are intended. We have an idea in England, for instance, that the driver of a vehicle is placed on the box for the purpose of guiding that vehicle, and that the reins are placed in his hand to enable him to direct the exertions of the horse; but such is by no means the case in Ceylon. He is there merely as a betel-chewing, expectorating peg on which the reins are suspended, but over which he exercises no control: he sits immovable, except as regards the whip-hand, which he uses most liberally going up hill, or through very deep ground: he never, for a moment, entertains any notion of guiding the horses, that office being undertaken by a miserable horsekeeper, who changes at each stage, and sits during the transit either on the foot-board behind, or on the step of the carriage; and whether the vehicle comes to grief by going up a bank on one side, or down a bank on the other, or into a train of waggons in front, appears to all whom it most nearly concerns a matter of utter indifference.

The distance to Colombo is some seventy miles, and the road throughout its entire length runs close to the sea, from which it is separated only by a thin belt of cocoa-trees. For the greater part of the distance both sides of the road are lined with native huts, little bamboo and talipot-leaf buildings, resembling those that usually adorn the illustrated editions of Paul and Virginia. So continuous is this line of buildings that the traveller almost fancies he is passing through some straggling suburb; and any person judging of the population of the island from the road between Galle and Colombo, would come to the conclusion that the island was one of the most denselypeopled, instead of being, as in reality it is, one of the most thinly-inhabited spots in the East. If the stranger is struck with the *number* of natives who throng the road-side, he is no less struck with their invariable listlessness and want of energy. The men seem to have no more urgent employment than lying at full length on mats or benches at the entrance of their huts, and gazing at the passers-by, or of squatting on their heels in rows, like frogs at the edge of a pool, masticating their chaw, and expectorating with a freedom and precision worthy of better men. The only energy indigenous to the country is shared in pretty equal proportions by the children and the pariāh dogs, who rush out, and shout and bark after the coach, much in the same way that the like "critters" do in more temperate climes. It appears to be an instinct, as universal as it is annoying, for the children of all countries, nations, and languages, to shout and use frantic endeavours to overtake passing vehicles, and for dogs to do so likewise.

The road was almost thronged with strings of curious little waggons, with arched talipot roofs projecting before and behind: these, drawn by the most diminutive of cattle, some actually not much higher than a large mastiff dog, and crawling unwillingly along at a steady rate of half-a-mile an hour, bore a strong resemblance at a short distance to huge snails dragging their slow length. The unbroken groves of cocoa-nut, for the distance of seventy miles, are more valuable to the proprietor than interesting or picturesque to the traveller. The land is of the average value of about 50*l.* per acre, and belongs exclusively to natives, who prepare those nuts they do not consume, for the Colombo oil-presses. The invariable tendency of the cocoa-nut to bend sea-wards is very remarkable on this road; notwithstanding the strength and continued prevalence of the sea-breeze, at least nine-tenths of the trees have a most decided inclination towards the ocean. They, together with the oyster-bearing mangroves of the West Indies, seem to thrive as well in salt water as in fresh: they court the spray, and in many instances you see healthy trees laden with fruit whose roots are washed and saturated by the waves. In fact these two species of trees may decidedly be classed under the head of Amphibia, if such an order exists in inanimate creation.

Your first five minutes in the Island of Ceylon impress you with the almost innumerable uses to which the cocoa palm is applied. The roofs of the huts, the screens from the sun, the mats, the drinking-cups, the ropes, in fact nearly every article of daily use, is the produce of this useful tree. It conduces scarcely less to the support than to the comfort of human life. The juice of the tree, when fresh drawn, affords a sparkling refreshing drink, very much resembling the pulque or toddy drawn from the American Aloe, in

South America; when fermented the toddy becomes arrack, by no means a nauseous, though an excessively intoxicating beverage. The nuts, when green, are filled with delicious milk, and when mature, supply a delicate food, though indigestible to any save school-boys or niggers. The cocoa-nut is to the native of Ceylon, what the date palm is to the Arab of the desert, and the eight hundred uses of the latter, and the hundred and eight of the former, have throughout ages been celebrated by the poets of both countries. When a grove of cocoa trees is in the course of being tapped for toddy, the drawers fasten three coir ropes from tree to tree, one to walk on, and one for either hand, and along these they pass with considerable rapidity. When seen at a short distance the ropes are invisible, and the curious effect is produced of a man crossing from tree to tree at a height of fifty or sixty feet from the ground, without any visible means of support.

As you approach Colombo, the road-side houses increase in number, and alternate rather prettily with the government cinnamon gardens that bound the road on either side. There is little doubt that cinnamon is the cassia of the Jews and ancients, and there seems a probability, from the remote ages to which the cultivation of this shrub can be traced in Ceylon, that it is the very place from which it was brought by Solomon's ships. The ancients did not know whence it came, and, like the topaz,* its habitat was for years a matter of wonder and speculation. In the days of Herodotus it was believed that some large birds in Arabia made their nests of branches of cassia, but whence they procured them was unknown. The means resorted to for securing these nests were rather original. The natives scattered large masses of flesh around, and the birds being of a greedy and selfish turn of mind, filled their nests with such quantities, that at length they gave way and fell to the ground—probably the original conception of the Roc in the history of Sindbad the Sailor.

The monopoly of cinnamon was guarded by the Dutch with some of the most iniquitous laws that even they, cruel and oppressive as they have always been in their commercial policy, ever enacted. To secure the monopoly to Ceylon, the entire growth of these trees in Java and the Coromandel coast was destroyed, the slightest peculation in the matter of exportation was followed by immediate death, and the smallest sprig of cinnamon was valued more highly than the limb of a human being. The consumption—for what reason, I know not—has of late years con-

* From τοπάζειν, "to wonder."

siderably decreased and the production is by no means so lucrative as formerly. Cinnamon is known to possess particular properties as an antidote to the destructive effects of mercury, and the miners and purifiers of the quicksilver mines in Mexico and South America consume by far the larger portion of the cinnamon crop in Ceylon. It flourishes in a sandy soil, and is a pretty shrub of some four or five feet high; the hue of the leaf and the form of the shrub reminding one considerably of a dwarf lilac. The work in a cinnamon garden between crop time is very light, consisting solely of weeding. The cutting and peeling is a very neat operation, and was formerly entirely confined to a low caste, amongst the Cingalese, whose sole occupation, one may almost say, information, lay in that science. There are three barks, of which the second or middle one only supplies the cinnamon of commerce. The monopoly of peeling is now however being gradually destroyed by the Malabar men from the coast, who are supplanting the inhabitants of Ceylon, much in the same way as the Norway rat has driven out the black rat in England, or as the Scotch settlers and Anglo-Americans have respectively supplanted the Celts of the North of Ireland, and the Aborigines of North America.

Colombo is about as hot and unpicturesque a

place as it has ever been my luck to visit; to the stranger there is neither object of interest or amusement, and but for the extreme kindness and easy hospitality of its merchants, it would puzzle the most contented mind to pass a week there without excessive ennui. There are, so to speak, three towns, one small and compact, situated within the Dutch fort, composed chiefly of government and merchants' offices, barracks, and shops, and two long straggling suburbs without the walls, stretching and stinking in opposite directions. A large fresh-water lagoon of a most green, slimy, tropical appearance, producing in abundance a lotus of almost Victoria Regia magnificence, stretches away to the back of the fort, and around it are situated the bungalows of many of the Colombo merchants. The propinquity of this lake would in any other tropical country (in the West Indies certainly) be considered as ensuring a considerable amount of fever to the neighbourhood; in fact, I doubt whether any advantage would be sufficient to induce a West Indian to locate in such a position. However, Ceylon, in the matter of climate, stands *per se*, and offers a total antithesis as regards the healthiness of certain districts to most other tropical countries. Whilst the vicinity of tanks and lagoons of the most fœtid and agueish character is perfectly healthy, that of rivers is equally deadly. This apparent contradiction of the usual laws of nature is accounted for by two reasons. The tanks are covered with various aquatic plants, which, by a kind Providence, are made to serve not only as filterers and purifiers of the water itself, but even as consumers of a considerable portion of the noxious exhalations, that would otherwise poison the neighbourhood. The banks of rivers, on the contrary, are rife with fever: the cause assigned for it is, that during the rainy seasons they swell to a great size, and collect the vegetable matter of a large extent of country, but owing to the rapidity with which they fall at the commencement of the dry season, and the winding and intricate nature of their course, the streams are unable to clear themselves, and this accumulation is left to decay in its bed, and infect the surrounding country. There exists also another reason—the beds of the Ceylon rivers are almost invariably composed of sand, and the stream, instead of sweeping down the decomposed vegetable matter it holds in its waters, as must be the case in hard-bedded rivers, percolates through the sand, leaving the poisonous matter on the surface exposed to the burning rays of the tropical sun.

CHAPTER III.

"DOBIES"—CHOLERA—MALABAR SERVANT—MOORMEN—"TATTOOS"—PUNCHY.

The anchorage for vessels of more than one hundred tons burden is very bad at Colombo, and except during the season of the coffee shipping, there are seldom more than one or two vessels lying there: being moreover quite out of the route of all the steamers, it does not share with Galle the excitement of witnessing the arrival and departure of old and new friends.*

The weather inside the fort, where every item of sea-breeze is excluded, is very oppressive, and, as a matter of course, the barracks of the European troops are situated in the very hottest part of it; and there, between two broad stagnant ditches, that hardly-used animal, the British soldier, may be seen daily keeping guard under a sweltering sun, in the very same tight coat, stiff stock, and heavy accoutrement, that he would

* There is, however, a considerable import trade carried on in the articles of coolies and rice from the mainland, but beyond the occasional stranding of one or two of these vessels with two or three hundred coolies, or two or three hundred tons of rice, on the "Drunken Sailor" or on the "Bar," the shipping interest is nil.

wear if standing sentry over silver foxes and Polar bears in the Arctic regions.

The hotels are of course execrable and expensive: the bed-room story was a large upper barn, that would have been flush, but for a number of very slight bulkheads which, not reaching above six feet from the floor, admitted a perfectly free circulation of air and conversation from one end to the other. The consequence of this arrangement was an intimate knowledge of all your neighbours' movements and occupations. This might occasionally be inconvenient, and I was excessively amused one morning by being, I can scarcely say the *unwilling* auditor of a most confidential, and to one party doubtless a most *interesting conversation*, between a lady, *young*, to judge by her voice, and *very young*, to judge by her sentiments, and her trusty *soubrette*. To my vexation, at the very instant the name of the dear creature whose whiskers and dancing I had heard so warmly and lovingly commented upon, was trembling on the timid lips of the fair inamorata, somebody at the other end of the house let a boot or a clothes' brush fall, and the word was lost.

It was at Colombo that I first became acquainted with the Anglo-Cingalese idiom. I had heard the "talkie talkie" of the niggers in Demarara, and the scarcely euphonious language of the

Egyptian boatmen and donkey boys, but such a wanton, deliberate perversion of grammar as the language spoken by the Cingalese was quite new to me, and striking from its boldness and originality. In all Eastern hotels the Dobies, or washermen, and the barbers wander about like tame cats, picking up indifferently a stray shirt or a stray beard. At Colombo their attentions were especially annoying, and almost made one in disgust foreswear clean chins and clean shirts for ever. In consequence of the excessive heat and the unceasing attacks of the mosquitoes, the night had generally reached the small hours before the feverish individual, exhausted and irritated with tossing from side to side, and provoked to a degree with unsuccessful attempts to discover the hole in the curtains that admitted all the mosquitoes, had attained any degree of calmness and resignation; at that delicious moment, when, more than half asleep, he had just counted the last "sheep round the corner," or the last rook flying over his head, he was sure to be aroused to full consciousness by a gentle tap most pertinaciously continued, accompanied by a "*Sar*" softly whispered through some chink in the door or partition. Directly the wretched creature heard by the discontented grunt within that the object of his persecution was awakened, he followed up his unwelcome interruption with, "Sar, Dobie come; Dobie want?" The ordinary means of repulsing an unwelcome intruder, by the use of strong language, and telling them in the elegant language of Sam Weller, "to go and be something unpleasanted," had no effect whatever on the Dobie; he was alike proof against threats and abuse, and it was only by dozing with a heavy boot close at hand, and discharging it with all one's force against the chink whence issued the small voice, that one had any chance whatever of again continuing one's slumbers. In consequence of the peculiar arrangement of the rooms I have mentioned, I could sometimes hear the Dobie and Barber commence their round at the extremity of the building, and, when not too much wearied, it was most amusing to hear the different tones of disgust with which they were received by the irate sleepers.

Notwithstanding the heat, Colombo is very healthy,—to my mind the most healthy place in the island; but during my first visit the cholera was more than ordinarily severe. As is so frequently the case with that strange malady, it seized, on its first appearance, some three or four of the strongest, and apparently least susceptible of the Europeans, and then confined itself entirely to the natives and the Malays. Its approach seemed to cause a greater panic than I had anticipated amongst Europeans accustomed to its presence, and amongst the natives, their excessive dread of the disease was alone enough to give it to them. The number of devils and sawncy's they propitiated with tom-toms and pipes, would have furnished a calendar of most portentous length.

Not relishing the notion of being attended upon by a Cingalese of uncertain gender, with a petticoat and high back comb, and hearing, moreover, from reliable sources that they were the most inveterate liars, scarcely speaking the truth even by accident, "we took up with," as housemaids say, a young man from the mainland; he was from the Malabar coast, and was so far better than the Cingalese, that, though he wore long hair, he concealed it with a turban, and though he *generally* wore a petticoat, he *occasionally* indulged in breeches. He was a Roman Catholic, and not a little proud of being of "same caste as master,—able to eat anything." His use of the vernacular, although far more grammatical than the Dobie, was interlarded with slang, in a manner that was occasionally most amusing. He would, for instance, ask me if I wanted my "swell" coat, when going out to dinner; and he told me one day, most confidentially, that my horse-keeper was "a stunner," though in what particular sense he did not explain. One morning, when he came into my room, I was quite taken aback by his saying, in a most serious tone, "Master, we did very wrong last night." Why? what happened? "We priggie one wipe," at the same time producing some stranger's handkerchief I had pocketed by mistake for my own. However, he was an excellent servant, and at the end of my stay in Ceylon I parted with him, without having detected any sin of a deadly nature in him.

As I said before, the Malabars are fast supplanting the Cingalese in their own country; and, in my opinion, it is a very good thing too, for a more miserable, effeminate, treacherous, lying, cowardly race than the low-country Cingalese, I believe do not exist: that is my opinion; however, I may be labouring under a mistake. They have all the bad qualities of the West Indian nigger, viz. their superciliousness and affectation, without any of the redeeming qualities of a cheerful, amusing disposition. The Malabar men (or "boys," as they are called from the age of seven to seventy) are, I think, good servants; but the Malay boys, of whom there are a great number, are said to be better,—that is, supposing they get attached to their masters; for, as they invariably carry their *creeses* or daggers about their persons, and have been known to use them on the slightest occasion, they can otherwise scarcely be esteemed agreeable body-servants. It is the height of a Malabar, Cingalese, or Malay boy's ambition to procure a good situation as dressing-boy or butler; and it is a curious fact that the only race who will not take service at any price, are the Moormen of the island, the most plodding and money-making of all the inhabitants.

This energetic race scorn all domestic employments, and confine themselves entirely to the occupations of hawkers, merchants, and carriers, owning bullocks and bullock-carts, and carrying loads and making their money by such like independent labour: they have in many instances amassed large fortunes, and are still doing so in an increasing ratio. In many parts of the island, especially in the south-eastern portion, the best Paddy districts and the best cocoa-nut plantations are invariably owned and cultivated by Moormen. Their history is, I believe, somewhat obscure, and it is not fully ascertained whether they came from the mainland after the Mahommedan conquest of India, or whether they are not the descendants of the old Egyptian and Arabian traders from the Red Sea, who supplied the Western World with ivory and cassia and other eastern products, long before the exact locality from whence they were derived was known to the consumers. I incline to the latter supposition, for in their person and energetic habits they display a much greater resemblance to the Fellahs of Egypt and the boatmen of the Red Sea, than they do to the luxurious and indolent Mussulmans of India: their constant intercourse with the Red Sea, and with the sacred localities of Mecca and Medina, would fully account for their having embraced the Mahommedan faith, of which they are now very strict followers.

After we had been in Colombo some ten or twelve days, we received a very kind invitation from the planters from the upper country, to accompany them on an elephant-shooting trip. I am not one of those who are so "excruciatingly" fond of shooting, probably from the fact of my being a very bad shot; and my ideas of sport are so closely connected with the sensation of being outside a horse, that I fairly confess I would any day rather have a rattling gallop over a good grass country, than slay all the elephants and pheasants in England or Ceylon. But it would never have done to have left the "Mother of Elephants" (as the island is called), without seeing some of her progeny in their wild state; and moreover, it offered an opportunity of testing the beauty of the island, which, if not Paradise itself, is, as Matthews said of Plymouth, "only three doors removed on the right hand side from it." We consequently accepted the invitation with pleasure, and immediately commenced an active search for *tattoos* or ponies.

Ceylon is not self-supplying in the matter of horse-flesh, but depends entirely upon foreign importation. Australia, the Cape, Persia, India, and Arabia, furnish the horses; Pegu, Sumatra, and the Deccan, the ponies. Of the latter, the Pegu pony is by far the most valuable, a good one fetching from 20*l.* to 30*l.*; they are very handsome, strong, well-plucked, and enduring. The exportation from Pegu is a strict monopoly, and the punishment of death is decreed, and I believe inflicted, on any natives who may assist in exporting mares, or who in any way facilitate the diffusion of the breed in foreign countries. Whether the conquest of Pegu will open the market I cannot say. The Australian and Cape horses are the finest animals, but they are seldom "well topped," and are almost invariably badly paced, badly broken, and badly mouthed. The Arab horses are neat hacks, but mere weeds, and go too close to the ground to be always agreeable. Altogether the horses in Ceylon are not of the first quality, and compared with Prussian, English, or American horses, are miserable specimens of the equine race. I don't think I saw a horse in the island that would have fetched 40*l.* at Tattersalls. A half-bred Arab or a good Mahratta tattoo, are the most agreeable and economical, and by far the most useful animals. We searched the stables and examined numerous steeds of various styles and sizes, but could not meet with anything that at all promised to be serviceable in a jungle trip. At length, as I was giving up the search in despair, and had made up my mind to trust to luck to supply me with some four-legged animal up country, I was fortunate enough to make the acquaintance of a gentleman lately returned from the jungle, and he offered to dispose of his pony to me, warning me at the same time that though very strong and hardy, he was rather a "headstrong animal:" however, as I infinitely prefer a wicked horse to one with no spirit whatever, I did not consider this any very great disadvantage; so after arranging about the price, &c., we proceeded to view the noble animal. He was not a "tartar of the Ukraine breed," but a pony of the Acheen breed, and a handsome one at that, combining a greater amount of strength in a smaller space than I have ever seen in a quadruped before: if he had been a hand and a half higher he would have fetched 100 guineas. He was a pony possessing a remarkably mild aspect, and standing in his stall, he really looked as if "butter would not melt in his mouth;"

but, when he was brought out, I could see by the watchful eye his horse-keeper kept on his movements, and by the alacrity with which the other horse-keepers "cleared out," that his master had not belied his disposition. However, as this was no particular object, and as in other respects he appeared the very animal I required, Punchy, (meaning a baby elephant, and by which name he was immediately christened,) together with his horse-keeper, bucket, and several small articles, became my property, for the sum of 11*l.* or 12*l.* Certainly the goddess Até must have presided in person over the birth of Mr. Punchy, and endued him *quintâ parte,* with the quintessence of her disposition, for it is impossible to conceive any animal, biped or quadruped, in whom the love of mischief was more irresistible: he was always at it, and could not be quiet for a single instant. If not engaged in biting some other horse, or chasing some unfortunate cooly to make him drop his load, he would amuse himself by trying to bite my foot and leg when I was not looking out: the only person he would do anything for *con amore* was his horse-keeper, the most patient and long-suffering of pariahs; and the incessant means of annoyance he practised on him, nipping his back, pulling his turban off his head, (a grievous insult to a Hindu,) treading on his heels, or dragging him at full speed across any open ground that presented itself, was enough to have enraged any other mortal. The man used indeed occasionally to look at me with a piteous imploring air, as if inquiring "what *am* I to do?" but I never once saw him strike or revenge himself on the pony in any way; and I feel convinced a considerable amount of affection existed between the two.

According to the Cingalese doctrine of metempsychosis, the spirits that have behaved badly in the human shape, are shifted into the form of some domestic animal, and those that have done well, into that of a wild animal; the most dreaded of all changes being that into a woman. If ever, in the course of these transmigrations, the spirit of Punchy animates the bulk and might of an elephant, he will be a "rogue" of the worst description, and I can only pity those sportsmen or villagers that chance to fall in his way. I have been thus tedious and particular in my description of Punchy and his peculiarities, as a very considerable amount of my amusement, as well as annoyance, during the trip, arose from his vagaries; and I am convinced the coolies will remember the "thin Sahib's" (as I was christened) pony, long after all remembrance of the "thin Sahib" himself has faded from their minds.

CHAPTER IV.

STAGE TO KANDY—RAILROADS—ROADS IN CEYLON—KANDY—MONSOONS.

We left Colombo without many regrets; for, as I before observed, but for the hospitality of its residents, it is as stupid a place as I ever visited. In travelling in the East, it is always considered advisable to start at some unnatural hour in the morning, and the Colombo and Kandy coach abided by that general rule. If the stage from Galle to Colombo was badly horsed, and the horses badly treated, that from Colombo to Kandy was a hundred degrees worse: more gross ignorance in the management of the noble animal itself, and more wilful cruelty, I never saw practised. In England I should have had the greatest satisfaction in handing over every driver and horse-keeper that drove and abused the horses during the ten or twelve stages from Colombo to Kandy, to the "Society for the Prevention of Cruelty to Animals," and I should have done so with a perfect confidence in their conviction.

A mile or two from Colombo the road crosses a bridge of boats over some river with an unpronounceable name; the tolls on the bridge clear between four and five thousand a-year, from the number of bullock-carts that pass over it, ascending with rice, and descending with coffee. A railroad from Kandy to Colombo has for years been mooted and discussed, and finally referred to the Home Government; it could not fail, I think, to be of immense service to the planters, as affording them the means of importing their rice and exporting their coffee at a much cheaper rate than at present.

I fancy no railroad has yet been constructed which has not greatly increased the traffic of the country through which it passes, and I think there can be little doubt that it would operate in the same beneficial manner in Ceylon. However, colonial statesmen are, in no part of the world that I am acquainted with, much famed for independence or celerity in legislation, and notwithstanding its being acknowledged on all hands that the railroad is a desirable undertaking, it is yet more than probable that, together with many other advantageous projects, it may be deferred to the Greek kalends. The rents of the bridges alone, amounting to several thousands of pounds, offer a very fair foundation on which to construct calculations for any amount of increase in the traffic.

For the first twenty miles the road is very flat, running through fields of paddy, and native villages, and cocoa groves, displaying the usual amount of children and pigs; the second twenty miles undulates through a mountainous and very picturesque country; and the last twenty, in which the road ascends some two thousand feet, almost approaches grandeur in its scenery. It certainly is a very beautiful drive, and if it was twenty, instead of seventy miles, it could not easily be exceeded; but seventy miles is too much, and long before the traveller has completed the first forty miles, exhausted nature begins to yearn and grumble, and when ascending the most beautiful part, one is, I am afraid, more apt to wonder how much longer the coach is to ascend at a foot's pace, and why on earth the engineers did not make the ascent easier, &c. &c., than to be enchanted and engrossed with scenery that, in reality, is most noble.

It has been very much the fashion of late years to extol the roads of Ceylon in comparison with those of India, and certainly there can be no doubt whatever of their immense superiority, both in extent and formation; but then it must be remembered that the two finest roads in the island, viz. that from Galle to Colombo, and that from Colombo to Kandy, made during the governorship of Sir Edward Barnes, were constructed entirely by *travaux forcés*, or impressed labour; a means of improvement and progress the government of India has never possessed. Surveyorships and inspectorships of roads are very popular appointments in Ceylon, and when one considers the number of the staff employed, and the amount of capital and jobbing engaged in that service, one sees that it could only be the result of the grossest possible negligence if the trunk lines were not good. You hear of men in difficulties, from extravagance or misfortune, having "taken to the road" much in the same language, only in a different sense, that broken-down gentlemen did some hundred years ago. A career on the Ceylon roads is, however, more certain in its profits, and does not necessarily finish up with a *pas seul* on the slack rope, *à la Claude Duval.*

In days gone by, the Cingalese were the unwilling pioneers of the splendid roads I have mentioned; and, though they must by this time be fully alive to their pecuniary advantages, it appears as though, in these days of liberty, they will not stir one finger, or give one pice, to keep them in order; this is done entirely by Malabar coolies, paid and organized by government. Out of the hundreds of coolies on the road from Colombo to Kandy, I did not see one Cingalese workman: the Cingalese are of that miserable race that will not work unless forced to do so. Even gold, that all-powerful persuader, fails in producing the desired effect; and I feel convinced, that if English energy and Malabar labour were removed, all that has hitherto been done for the island would, in five years, have utterly and entirely disappeared, and the coffee and cocoa crops have sunk to nothing.

The Maha-neura, or great city, now called Kandy, is very prettily situated at the broad end of a pear-shaped lake, which almost fills the valley, formed by some very picturesque and striking hills. The forms of these hills, clothed with rank verdure to their summit, and the tortuous shape of the lake when seen from several points of view, reminded us very strongly of Westpoint, on the Hudson river. The Maha-villajanga, or River of Sand, surrounds three parts of the city, at the distance of from two to four miles: this river is very beautiful, some of its reaches almost grand, but I do not believe its clear rushing stream adds much to the salubrity of Kandy. The views in the immediate neighbourhood are excessively pretty; and at the distance of a mile or two, when the hills that immediately surround the basin in which the town is placed, are surmounted, the bird's-eye view of the distant country, backed by the bold, thickly-wooded mountains, alone repays a long pilgrimage. The view from Lady Horton's walk, a spiral drive round one of the surrounding hills, and for which the inhabitants of Kandy are indebted to the wife of Sir Wilmot Horton, is especially beautiful, and is remarkable as uniting in one *coup d'œil* the characteristics of one of the most rainy and one of the most parched countries in the world.

I am not aware of any country that presents such opposite peculiarities of climate as Ceylon, or in which an admirer of continual moisture, or unbroken drought, could so easily suit himself. The island is swept alternately by the south-west and north-east monsoons, each of which remain in full force for six months; but the south-west monsoon, saturated with the enormous evaporation from the tropical ocean and the supposed wet land of Abyssinia, brings far more rain than the north-east monsoon; in fact, the rain in some parts of the island during the time it prevails is incessant. After discharging abundant moisture in its south-westerly course, it is at length intercepted at its rain-level by the mountains of the interior, and completely emptied of its moisture, and thence it continues its course indeed over the north-east part of the island, but with the material difference of having totally changed its nature from a cold and saturating, to a dry and almost parching wind. In November, the north-east monsoon commences to blow, and continues during five or six months, but in consequence of its having traversed far cooler seas and drier lands than the south-west monsoon, it bears comparatively little moisture; and the rain does not extend beyond the mountains of the interior: so that whilst the south-west half of the island has six months fine weather, and is saturated for the other six, the north-east portion has ten months consecutive, unbroken, fine weather, during which not a drop of rain falls, and only two months moisture. This peculiarity of the monsoon may account for the fact of all the tanks, the gigantic nature of which render Ceylon so interesting as telling of bygone wealth and prosperity, being situated in the north-east portion of the island. Standing on Lady Horton's walk during the south-west monsoon, and looking towards the north-east, you can distinguish the line in the clouds distinctly marked where the rain ceases abruptly. And whilst the hills and mountains immediately around you are rank and reeking with excessive moisture, the background is filled up with mountains that for ten months scarcely see rain, displaying those hazy roseate tints that constitute so peculiar a beauty in Italian scenery, and that tell plainly of a parched soil cropping out through a stunted and scanty vegetation.

In the centre of the lake which borders the town, is placed a low massive building of some sixty or seventy feet in length, now converted into a magazine for warlike stores; and certainly, surrounded entirely by water, it offers as suitable a place for the safe preservation of the munitions of war as can well be imagined. In the days of the kings of Kandy it was used as a magazine for different, though scarcely less inflammable materials, and witnessed, I imagine, more explosion of passion and agony than it is ever likely to see of shells and fusées. It was the Royal Agapemone, the residence of the female favourite for the time being: and thither the kings retired to enjoy the combined delights of betel and female society, apart from the crowd and jealousy of their more luxurious zenana. Removed from all possibility of interruption, and with a quarter of a mile of water all round, its situation offered powerful and almost unanswerable arguments against the pride or obstinacy of those obdurate beauties to whom the royal wishes were not law. The water was too deep and too close at hand to allow of much parleying; it was a word and a splash, and all was over, and a canoe sent across the water for a fresh beauty. These waters of the lake afforded to the kings of Kandy a more convenient and instantaneous quietus to those whose beauty had sated, or whose reproaches were tiresome, than even the Nile and the Bosphorus to the rulers of Turkey and Egypt

The Kandians fought well for their kings, and exhibited a considerable amount of loyalty both in their defence of them, and in their blind obedience to their grievous tyrannies; but it is curious that, notwithstanding the invariable faith with which they applied the healing unction of "the divine right of kings" to their crushed liberties and mutilated persons, their rulers should invariably have been foreigners, elected from some of the Tamul princes on the Malabar coast. These princes were maintained in their sovereignty by no foreign aid, but entirely by the unanimous obedience of those by whom they were elected. Whether this obedience arose from a tacit conviction of their own inability to rule themselves, or from their own strife and dissensions, I cannot take upon myself to say; but though their first defence appears to have been stubborn and even successful, they soon bowed their necks to the yoke of the stranger, and endured without complaint much the same treatment from the Tamul as our forefathers did from their Norman invaders.

CHAPTER V.

TAMUL PRINCES—INSURRECTION OF 1848—LORD TORRINGTON POLICY—BUDDHIST PRIEST.

The cruelty and oppression of these kings, up to the time of their overthrow by the British, in the present century, was incredibly barbarous; and no history that I am acquainted with, not even that of Imperial Rome, contains narrations of such unnatural and systematic brutality. Mothers engaged in the pleasing task of pounding their offspring to death in mortars; state prisoners buried up to the neck, with the king and his friends playing at bowl at their heads, till some fortunate blow deprived the wretched sufferers of life: elephants treading criminals to death; impalements and disembowelings, were, if the old chronicles are to be believed, of every day occurrence in the capital, and excited no excessive enmity or disgust on the part of the πολλοὶ, against their foreign rulers. The descendants of these kings still exist; but though pensioned by Govern ment, they are not allowed to reside in the island.

The hereditary nobility, the Kandy chiefs as they are called, still remain, and exercise considerable influence over their followers; they are nearly all pensioners under the British Government, and their former rank and position recognised under the term of headsmen. However, the sop of 60*l.* a-year, although, of course, acceptable, does not by any means console them for their departed glory and diminished importance; and their injured pride and smouldering hatred of British rule are, I believe, but indifferently concealed.

This feeling of enmity long smothered, broke out lately, causing the much vexed insurrection of 1848. The object of the conspiracy, to which nearly all the headsmen were pledged, was the utter destruction and expulsion of the British settlers and troops, and the reassumption of hereditary power by the chiefs themselves. The plans were secretly and carefully matured, under the blessing and encouragement of the priesthood; and the annual feast of the Pirahara, which takes place in August or September, was fixed upon as the moment for making the attempt in Kandy itself, and was intended to have been simultaneous with risings in the other portions of the Kandian country. The indiscretion of some of the principal rebels, and a certain want of unanimity unavoidable in any revolt conducted under numerous leaders, caused the miscarriage of what might otherwise have been an insurrection of very serious moment; and, indeed, sufficient disturbances did take place to demonstrate very clearly that their open threats of burning, impaling, and exterminating, were not mere words of bravado: one Englishman was brained on the high road, not two miles from Kandy, and another was only saved from the culinary attentions of a party of natives, who tried to roast him, by the fortuitous arrival of a body of troops. The Kandian rebellion of 1848 seems to bear considerable resemblance to that of Ireland, under Smith O'Brien, about the same period; in both cases the bloodthirsty disposition of the majority was well ascertained, and the isolated, defenceless position of the well disposed equally recognised. In either case, the difficulty of getting reliable information was very great, and the power and resources of the discontented imperfectly known; and, as a matter of course, greatly exaggerated. The battle in the cabbage garden, on Boulagh Common, fought by twelve policemen and a few scores of half-starved peasants, put an end to the one, and the timely appearance of a handful of troops at Matura suppressed the other; but who can affirm that in either case if any mishap had occurred, or if the collisions had not actually taken place at the very time they did, serious and bloody riots might not have broken out?

I believe there is little doubt that there were many instances of bad faith amongst Government officials, during the riots of 1848, in Ceylon; and whether from incompetence or wilfulness, many and serious misrepresentations did occur; but although, in England, the offences were laid on the wrong shoulders, in Ceylon itself the truth is better known, and the contempt and scorn of all honest persons is the only reward their double dealing has secured to them.

The planters, whose lives and properties were especially jeopardized during the revolt, have given unmistakeable evidence of their opinion of Lord Torrington's conduct during the whole affair, by presenting him with a piece of plate as a grateful acknowledgment of his energy and decision during that trying season, which alone saved them from imminent danger and ruin. Lord Torrington was blamed for being hasty, and for carrying into execution the sentences of the courts-martial with more severity than the establishment of martial law actually necessitated. Facts have, however, proved, that it is fortunate the executive took that view of the matter; the revolt, met with decision and nipped in the bud, was contemptible, while, if dallied with, and allowed to gain any head whatever, it could only have been suppressed with much bloodshed, and after the perpetration of disgraceful atrocities. What do the philanthropists of England know of the crafty, cruel nature, and bitter hatred of the Kandians; of the isolated positions of the planters, separated from each other by distances of many miles; or of the enormous amount of capital which even an unsuccessful revolt must have seriously affected? The fact is, there exists in England a party, strong in talents and weighty in counsel, Pecksniffian in their professions, "dénigreurs" in their actions, who, like the Athenian of old, who ostracised Aristides, merely because he was tired of hearing him always called the "Just," attack and condemn all those who in distant lands, and in perilous seasons, exercise to the best of their powers that independence of judgment, without the free use of which, responsibility can only be a farce. What purpose does it serve to appoint a man to a situation of trust and importance, if, the moment he exercises the energy and decision for which he has been selected, his conduct is to be animadverted upon, and blackened, by a number of carping, envious demagogues?

There is something so very un-English in the conduct of these men, and their philosophy is so palpably meretricious, that it is almost incredible that amongst a straightforward people, as we are supposed to be, and in a land where fair-play is accounted a national jewel, such conduct should be tolerated for one second. However, the British public,—endued, doubtless, with a more than average amount of national stability and common sense, as regards ordinary topics,—are, in the case of personal accusations, too much inclined to drop that golden maxim of our judicial code, viz. that every man is innocent till he is proved guilty; and, resigning their own right of judgment, to follow pell-mell some immaculate bell-wether, who thinks himself called upon to accuse. The persecution of Strafford and Warren Hastings, of Byng, and Lord Melville, have plainly shown that what by the gentle public is generally supposed to be a national impeachment and condemnation, is to those actually "le dessous des cartes," nothing more noble than personal malice or political animosity.

The principle of Don Cæsar de Bazan, that a lie, though only circulated for five minutes, may be of advantage to a cause; or the saying of Prince Talleyrand, that a lie that has had five minutes' circulation will take fifty years to contradict, is the dastardly policy that has met with but too many supporters in political accusations, and is the last resource of the public accuser, that necessary agent, contemptible at all times, but especially so when his ungracious offices are uncalled for, or when his philanthropy is blazoned forth to mask less worthy motives.

There is but too much reason to suspect that even Burke was a disappointed dabbler in East India stock, and that he saw in Warren Hastings not so much the agent of corruption and the oppressor of humanity, as the means by which his golden dreams had miscarried: and it is no less a matter of grave suspicion, that the independent conduct of Sir James Brooke, in refusing to countenance an Eastern Archipelago bubble,—a Company composed of men of straw,—has raised up a body of accusers, whose humanity is sharpened by envy, and their patriotism increased by disappointed covetousness.

The lies circulated about the Buddhist priest who was executed at Kandy, were at once the offspring of personal dislike and of popularity-seeking philanthropy. The priest was arrested in the very act of administering to hundreds of rebels an oath of enmity and revenge against the British inhabitants. If individual treason is a capital offence, he deserved death; if exciting a nation to revolt is criminal, he doubly deserved it; and if debasing and misapplying the influence of his priestly office could add to his crime, he had trebly earned his fate. The account of his being shot in his robes,—which was compared to shooting the Pope or the Archbishop of Canterbury in full canonicals,—was simply a fabrication, which designing men saw might be foisted upon the British public, whose ignorance of Cingalese customs might lead them to suppose that the priest's robe was that only used in religious ceremonies, and that the degradation of the national faith was as much the object of the government as the individual punishment of the traitor himself. Such, however, was not the case; the Buddhist priests don the saffron robe on entering the priesthood, or rather on becoming students, and never lay it aside till they retire from the service, or till they quit their human form for that of a cobra or an elephant. They have no other article of dress whatever, and if the priest had been deprived of that, he must have been exposed quite naked, degraded and disgraced, before all his people.

The punishment of treason was inflicted on him by a military court, and he would have suffered equally, whether he had been a Brahmin or a Mahommedan, a Protestant or a Roman Catholic. He was tried and executed in the dress in which his crime was committed. Do we suppose that those who lynched the Monk Clement, or shot the preachers of the Scotch covenant, waited to divest them of their ordinary attire, or intended to degrade the faith while they punished the traitor?

Not only was Lord Torrington perfectly warranted in acting as he did, but he would have had ample reason on his side had he forfeited the whole of the Buddhist property in the island.

Ceylon, as is of course well known, is the Lanka-dwipa, the Holy Land of the Buddhist, where, according to the best authority, flourished Gautama, the founder of their faith, and which now contains all their most venerated relics. The antiquity and exact origin of Buddhism has been a *quæstio vexata,* about which doctors have differed, do differ, and probably will continue to differ. Whilst by some it is supposed to be a Reformed creed, the successful effort of a numerous people to free themselves from the tyranny of castes and traditions that trammeled their faith, and to bear, in fact, much the same relation to the faith of Brahma, as the Christian religion did to that of the Jews; others, on the contrary, give it a far higher antiquity than any existing religion, and maintain that the Hindu faith is in reality the religion of Buddha, loaded with the impurities and tyranny that a powerful and ambitious line of priests have introduced.

Whatever may have been its former excellence,

I am afraid it has in the present age considerably deteriorated; and though scarcely so debasing as the Hindu religion, it is equally contemptible, and equally conducive to the moral and physical degradation of its followers. It is impossible, with any truth, to style *that* a religion which ignores the existence of any supreme Being whatever, and that inculcates the doctrine that after death the five elements composing the earthly tenement of the perfect, dissolve never to reunite, whilst those of the imperfect assume some other form;—that, amongst other comforting doctrines, teaches that *pleasure* is the grand object of life; that acts of piety, charity, and abstinence are unprofitable; that the body is the only real good, and should be worshipped, and that pleasant food, fine clothes, and handsome women, form the grand felicity of man; in support of which Sybarite philosophy, their founder indulged in an establishment of forty thousand concubines, beating King Solomon "hard held." One can only regard it as a debased and debasing school of heathen philosophy, and cannot be surprised that any nation guided by such promiscuous principles should have so utterly and hopelessly lost every sense of that morality, public and private, that in some degree, however slight, is generally supposed to leaven the lump of human depravity. You might, to make use of a Cingalese proverb, as wel. try "to turn a black crow into a white crane," or to make an "elephant pass through the spout of a kettle," as to instil the slightest conception of "a moral sense" into a Buddhist.

Notwithstanding the impossibility of reconciling conflicting testimonies, so as to form any conclusive theory as to the original date of Buddhism, the date of Guatama, the avatar or incarnation that is deified in Burmah and Ceylon, is, I believe, established on sufficient evidence. Books and traditions assert that he made his appearance in Ceylon some five or six centuries B.C., and was gathered, after a most abstemious and praiseworthy existence, at the ripe age of eighty. His last appearance as Guatama was much in the style of Grimaldi or Flexmore; he is described as having ears to his waist, hands reaching down to his knees, and to have come on the world's stage throwing summersaults, when, sticking his tongue in his cheek, we may suppose he squatted down with the "Here we are again!" It was nothing new to him, as he had appeared in the world 300 times before!

It must always be rather a difficult matter to explain the Buddhist philosophy, inasmuch as those who profess and hold by that creed, do not themselves understand it, and cannot therefore give any very lucid explanation of it to others. However, for those curious in the matter of Heathen theological philosophy, the following peculiarities may be interesting. Buddhism does not acknowledge any original creation of the world, but asserts that it has always existed, but has been destroyed and reproduced several times. Twenty-two regenerated worlds are enumerated, each in its turn successively governed by Buddhas. The present world has been governed by four Buddhas, of whom Guatama is the last and fourth. His doctrines prevail in Ceylon, Burmah and Siam. A fifth, Maitree Buddha, is yet to come, and is, I suppose, *"the coming man,"* so long expected. They imagine the earth was destroyed by fire, and revivified by water: rather reversing the order of our faith.*

After death, the worthy Guatama was supposed

* The beneficial effects of water in the history of this world, and in the history of their gods, seems to be a very general impression in the East, and the "Spirit of God moving upon the face of the waters" is fully realized in all heathen mythologies.

From the earliest days there appears to have been some very general system of worship of aquatic plants. The most ancient coins represent the tamara as sacred; the Japanese believe that Bromna, the eldest son of their chief god, was created on the tamara; the Egyptians represent Iris on the lotus; Krishna, the god of love amongst the Hindus, is represented as floating down the Ganges on one of the nymphæa, occupied in the infantine amusement of sucking his toe.

to have been absorbed, body and soul, into a divine essence, which is an indefinite object of Buddhist faith, most impossible to explain to any one not previously understanding it. This divine essence exerts no influence on the inhabitants of the world, either for good or evil, but possesses the power of absorbing the souls of all those who have attained perfection, and will, in the course of time, unite in its *perfect* essence all the good that is now, and has been, scattered amongst the inhabitants, since the world was first peopled. If any one can understand and explain the Buddhist faith from this, he must be a man of genius or imagination.

CHAPTER VI.

KANDY—IDOL IN THE GROVE—METEMPSYCHOSIS—PECULIARITY OF BUDDHIST PRIESTHOOD.

Kandy is to the Buddhists in some slight degree what Mecca is to the Mussulmans, and what Jerusalem was to the early Christians: there flourished the founders of their faith, and there are now cherished their most sacred relics. Here you see the idolatrous temple, and the "idol in the grove," the raising of which was in early days so deadly a sin, that for the commission of it Asa removed his mother Maachah from being queen. Amongst other relics in this far-famed "Temple of the Tooth," is the identical grinder of Buddha himself; at least so the priests say, but they do, and every one who cares can, know that the original tooth was destroyed by Constantine de Braganza in the year 1560, who, in revenge for the martyrdom of 600 of St. Francis Xavier's followers, burnt villages and temples, and made it his especial business to destroy the tooth. The present masticator is doubtless that of some more recent saint, or more probably of his human prototype, the ape; however, be that as it may, the Buddhists of India and China hold it in exceeding reverence, and an enormous treasure was offered by the priesthood of Siam for its possession.

I believe it is allowed by scholars as an undoubted fact, that the Beth-shan of the men of Jabesh-Gilead, from whence David rescued the bodies of Saul and Jonathan, signified the "Temple of the Tooth," and has been adduced by some as a proof of the exceeding antiquity of the Buddhist faith. But whatever may have been the nature of the idolatry of the men of Jabesh-Gilead, their worship could not well have been paid to the identical grinder, that in Buddhist countries has during so many centuries excited unceasing veneration. Guatama Buddha flourished between 500 and 600 B.C., whereas Saul and Jonathan met their deaths nearly 400 years before. However, as Booddhs had in other forms frequented the earth during many centuries, the "Temple of the Tooth" mentioned in Scripture may allude to a tooth that had seen service in some former incarnation.

Metempsychosis, or the transmigration of souls, is one of the most striking of the Buddhist tenets, as it is of some castes of Hindus. Although, to the reasoning mind, enlightened by revelation, this conception is in the highest degree degrading and ridiculous, it is yet very easy to trace out the chain of reasoning, starting from imperfect knowledge, by which it was established. It is founded on the system nature invariably follows in the vegetable world. The tree dies; from its decay springs fresh vegetation, whose corruption in turn supplies its successors. And thus the vital principle, at first confined to the tree itself, is renewed, and flourishes in successive developments. Every child has read with delight the "Transmigrations of Indur," and pictured to himself the delights of animal life, of being in turn a dormouse or an elephant, a monkey or a Solan goose; in maturer years, one is almost pleased at finding a people who actually believe all that we fancied was imagination,—it is like verifying the relations of Gulliver, or the adventures of Sindbad.

The doctrine of the transmigration of souls, in several modifications, has existed from very remote ages. The ancients believed that the souls of the good, after spending a certain number of years in Elysium, drank of the waters of Lethe, and, forgetting all they had suffered in a former existence and had enjoyed in Elysium, left that abode of bliss by the ivory gates, and entered into a new existence. The early Germans also believed in the transmigration of souls, varying this creed, however, with ideas of a gross Paradise of immortal drunkenness.

The Cingalese faith in Metempsychosis is entire and unhesitating, and their confidence in its truth admits of no doubt whatever. A man, when oppressed by his superiors, or condemned by the judge, expresses his intention of returning in a future state, as a cobra, to bite his children; or as an elephant, to ravage his crops. They even go so far as to form an opinion from the nature and habits of any particular animal or insect, as to its character in a former state. A Pariah dog, for instance, whose presence is an abomination, and whose portion is misery, is supposed to have been some luxurious Dives, who is now in want and ill-treatment, expiating his indifference of the Lazari of his human acquaintance; and there is a little insect very common in the jungle, which, from its remarkable habit of surrounding itself with a covering of small sticks, in the centre of which it moves, and from which it is almost impossible to distinguish it, is believed by the natives to represent individuals who, during their earthly career, displayed rather a marked partiality for their neighbours' fire-wood, and who are thus working out an appropriate atonement; a theory of future punishment rather in accordance with some of Dante's visions in the Purgatorio.

The bodies of all domestic animals are supposed to be tenanted by disgraced human souls, and as the object of their being thus brought into contact with their own species in an altered state, is that they may thus receive their proper amount of punishment, the Cingalese have a specious excuse for indulging their cowardly natures, and exercising the most beastly cruelty towards all their domestic dependants.

There is nothing very remarkable in the high temple at Kandy, and, compared with the ruins of former temples and places of worship, it is on a very small scale. It was entered during the rebellion of 1848, by the 15th Regiment, and the drums that were captured with Major Davie's party in 1818, were rescued. The possession of these drums was almost as much a matter of congratulation as that of the Tooth itself, and their loss was deeply deplored: however, the actual proofs of their successful treachery have been supplied by a pair of imitation drums, which, though more resembling children's toys than martial instruments, yet serve to keep alive the remembrance of former success, and to foster hopes of future vengeance.

As Kandy is the head-quarters of Buddhist

relics and superstition, so it is also of Buddhist learning and priestcraft. A college for the instruction of the priesthood has flourished for many centuries in the neighbourhood, and comprises nearly all the wise men of the island. The priesthood, or rather the expounders of the Buddhist Philosophy, is not, like the Brahmin or priestly caste in India, hereditary, nor must they of necessity belong to one particular caste: but on the contrary, the assumption of the priestly office is entirely optional, and open to all castes alike. The rules that ostensibly bind the priest so long as he wears the saffron robe are very severe, and if strictly adhered to should produce the most perfect priesthood the world has known; but, as is not unfrequently the case in other religions, the practice differs considerably from the profession. Celibacy is strictly enjoined, and, as in some Roman Catholic orders, the priests are bound to abstain from all labour, and to subsist entirely on the alms of the charitable. This latter injunction, intended, doubtless, as a means of mortification and humility, has given rise to a system of idleness and luxury which bears some resemblance to the monastic bodies of the middle ages.

There is one peculiarity in the Buddhist priesthood which is shared by no other order that

I have ever heard of, viz. the power that they possess, at any moment, of laying aside their profession of sanctity and their regulations, and of returning to the state and liberty of laymen. A priest who gets a little bored with his celibacy or his abstinence pledge, can doff his saffron robe and go out "on the loose" for a few weeks or months, and then return to his priestly duties.

There is little doubt that most priesthoods might be considerably purified by the retirement of those who feel themselves unfit for the office. Chaucer, who seldom philosophizes without cause, observes:—

> "Sith that a monk, when he is reckless,
> Is like a fish that is waterless;"

and no fish without water can be more entirely out of his element than one in holy orders against his will.

CHAPTER VII.

BUDDHIST SECTS—MISSIONARY LABOUR—FEAST OF THE PIRAHARA—MUSIC—THE KANDIAN LADIES—THEIR PREDILECTION FOR CHEWING—POLYGAMY—INFANTICIDE.

As the observance of the moral virtues, which we consider one of the chief of Christian duties, is scarcely recognised by the Cingalese, and is supposed only to apply to the officiating ministers of their idolatry, a priest does not in any way lose caste by joining in their immoralities or indulgences, so long as his impurity does not affect his ministry. There is something very striking in the appearance of a Buddhist priest in his ample saffron robe and his closely shaven head; and the habit adopted by the Siamese sect, of shaving the eyebrows, gives an expression to the eye that is anything but agreeable.

Like most other forms of faith, the Buddhist religion has its schism, which, though quiescent at present, was in former days the fruitful source of cruelty and persecution. The distinctions of caste were not recognised by Guatama, and in several of the Buddhist writings they are strictly prohibited. The Siamese sect, however, upheld that institution, and numbers of the Cingalese favouring their principles, resorted to Siam or Burmah to be educated and ordained. The Siamese sect are thus composed of high caste men, and the Amarapoora sect, or those educated at Amarapoora, in Ceylon, are of any caste whatever. The distinction between them now, however, is chiefly shown in slight peculiarities of dress; and their disputes as to whether the right or left shoulder should be left uncovered, or whether the eyebrows should be shaved or not, are about as edifying and nearly as sensible as the disputes about surplices, or stone altars, in our own Church.

Caring little about their own religion, and still less about any other, the Buddhists have, ever since the days of St. Thomas, offered a fair field for Missionary labours. A Primate of India was present at the Council of Nice, A.D. 325; therefore, it is probable that Christianity had extended to Ceylon even in that early age; but the perfect *insouciance* which exists about all religion, is the very thing that always has and always will offer an elastic opposition to proselytism, which no energy will ever overcome.

Mr. Hume's remark, that the "most refined and philosophic sects are constantly the most intolerant," is only half true in the case of

Buddhism. Their belief is scarcely refined, but it is essentially philosophical, and yet they are perfectly ready to tolerate any other, or to unite it with their own. The career of the sincere Missionary is consequently one of bitter and ever-recurring disappointments; (I do not now speak of those who become Missionaries from interested motives, and whose relations of conversions and victories in the spiritual warfare are, to any one who has visited the scenes of their exertions, as unfounded as they are mischievous.) They enter upon their good work full of energy and confidence; they find their services attended by willing hearers, their doctrines and explanations assented to by professed converts, and it is not till after precious years have been wasted, that they discover that they have been preaching to the winds; their doctrines and their words are not indeed blown back into their faces, but conveyed away by the gentle breezes of indifference, without fertilizing, or leaving any sign behind; and they are at length unwillingly convinced that their efforts would have been equally successful, had they expounded the dogmas of Mahomet, or the philosophy of Confucius.

The Cingalese will attend chapel, listen with attention, and apparently assent with understanding, but he will go from chapel to his idol, from the preaching of Christianity to the abominations of his degrading profession, without the slightest trace of change effected. It is an ungrateful office to decry the efforts of Missionaries in foreign countries, especially amongst savages and uneducated natives, but still it is undeniably the duty of travellers to offer the fruits of their experience, gathered in the several parts of the world they may have visited, and to expose the almost utter uselessness of a system that deprives the mother country of the energies of some of the most zealous and noble of her children, and squanders sums that, if expended at home, would bring to perfection fruit that has been implanted on good soil, but from neglect and want of attention is suffered to rot and perish.

My experience, gathered from visits amongst the Indians of North and South America, the Arabs of Asia, and the natives of Ceylon and India, and supported by the testimony and opinion of unprejudiced persons, whose long residence amongst them had made them acquainted with all their habits, leads me to believe, that scarcely one real convert, whose belief is sincere and lasting, annually rewards the labours of the hundreds who are engaged in the spiritual warfare. This opinion may appear incredible, and too frightful to be believed, and Exeter Hall would decidedly crush any one who ventured to assert such a fact, but two instances will prove that it is not entirely without foundation. The Abbé Dubois, who was for upwards of fifteen years the most energetic and enlightened of Roman Catholic Missionaries in India, declared when leaving that country, that during the whole period of his labours, he had not made one sincere Christian. A Baptist Missionary I visited in the Sioux country, told me that during thirteen years of uninterrupted residence and labour among the Indians, in which time he had educated scores of children, and translated two or three of the Gospels, he could not say that he had made one single convert whose profession was sincere. If the humane and Christian population of England would only inquire into these things, and instead of wasting their energies and their means in useless attempts to convert the heathen, whose time is not yet come, would unite to convert the heathen at home, they would find their labour crowned with certain success instead of as certain disappointment. Should we consider that man wise, who, deserting a fruitful soil at his own door, where every instant of labour would be repaid a hundred-fold, should expend his energies and his life in vain attempts to cultivate the sands of the Desert, or the icebergs of the Pole? Should we not rather look upon him as foolishly wasting those talents which were intended to be turned to better account? Yet such is the actual case of most of our missionary establishments. I know this assertion will be denied and scouted at by many interested persons, and by hundreds and thousands whom benevolence and a too confiding Christianity will not suffer to be convinced; but travellers will not deny it, and be only too ready to affirm its truth.

In Ceylon and in India, the Protestant Church has no chance in competition with the Roman Catholic. The importance of the precept, *In veste varietas sit, non sit scissura*, is fully recognised by the latter Church, which admits of no schism to affect its form of worship, thereby offering a marked contrast to the varied forms and conflicting doctrines of the Protestant faith, that, opposed with bitterness and intolerance, not only weaken and nullify her at home, but utterly confuse and astound the ignorant heathen abroad. How can an uneducated native discriminate between the profession of Presbyterians and Episcopalians, Baptists and Unitarians, or how can he suppose that the ministers of these different denominations, squabbling and opposing each other, can possibly be animated by any one universal belief? The Roman Church, moreover, recognises the doctrine of allowing the end to justify the means, and does not hesitate to tolerate and even patronise a certain admixture of idolatry in her worship—by that means inducing a belief among her converts, that the dissimilarity is not so great after all, and that by transferring their faith from Buddha to some other saint, whose image is offered to their worship, they are merely worshipping him in another form.

I have frequently entered Roman Catholic chapels in Ceylon, and seen the priest seated on high at the altar, surrounded by trashy finery and blazing lamps, receiving the grovelling prostrations of the worshippers, and it could not fail to strike me that the ceremony appeared too much like the adoration of the priest himself, the substitution of an animate for an inanimate object, —and that the idol-worship of the Buddhist, and the priest-worship of the Roman Catholic, were but different forms tending to the same end. The Roman Catholic Missionaries follow the policy of the Spanish Inquisition who accompanied Pizarro, and who, preferring force to persuasion, drove the miserable Peruvians by hundreds to the lakes and rivers, and, distorting those forcible immersions into genuine baptisms, sent home glowing accounts of the success that attended their noble efforts. The absurdity and falsehood of many missionary reports of the present day are scarcely less glaring and palpable. However, this is an ungrateful theme, and eloquence on such a subject as missionary labours is so easy, and can be made so noble, and people require so little proof in support of what they already believe, that it will require many years and many facts, and the evidence of a far greater number of travellers, to prove to England that her treasures, which might afford the blessings of Christianity and education to the thousands at home, are being wasted and misapplied in distant lands, and to convince her that you may as well expect Christianity to precede civilization, as that an oak will grow where there is no soil, or that the summer will precede the spring.

During a second visit to Kandy on my return, I had the fortune to be present during the most sacred and most strictly observed of all the Buddhist feasts; not that it was either amusing or instructive, but still, from my knowledge of it, I was enabled to judge of the truth of the accounts of others. It is called the feast of the Pirahara, and extends over a period of seven or eight days; the processions and public part of the business commence after dark, and continue nearly the whole night. I inquired of the best local authority, but could hear no very distinct explanation of its origin or intention. From what

I could gather, however, I imagine it is some kind of propitiatory offering to the God of rain, whose kind offices are expected about that season. The most effective part of the play appeared to me to consist in the parading backwards and forwards of seven elephants, decked in all kinds of tawdry ornaments, carrying howdahs, in which was nothing visible to the uninitiated, followed by crowds of men bearing palankeens, also empty; they were followed by some hundreds of headmen and chiefs, all attired in their best, and cheered, or rather stunned, by an accompaniment of tom-toms and pipes.

Music, the *regina sensuum*, as she is termed, has not, in our meaning of the word, extended her queenly sway over the East, for a more intolerable and hideous discord than the church music of the Hindu and Buddhist temples in India and Ceylon, it is impossible to conceive. These concerts commenced every day exactly at our dinner hour, and utterly interrupted the flow of soul which is usually supposed to be a concomitant of that sociable meal. "The concert of musicians at a banquet," may, indeed, "be like a carbuncle set in gold," but the musicians of King Solomon must have had a little stronger appreciation of melody than those of Kandy.

In the procession I observed several Fakeers

(men who try to establish a character for holiness by public exhibitions of torture and self-mortification), one of whom had certainly taken the most efficient means for displaying his efforts in the cause of sanctity, by conduct that showed that he had no need of the warning about placing his light under a bushel: he had run a stick or wire through both his cheeks, and stuck a lighted candle at each extremity, at the distance of about six inches from his face; it had a very disgusting appearance, but from the earnest manner in which he attracted our attention to it, I have no doubt it was considered a work of especial merit.

The high caste Kandians are very jealous regarding their hereditary dress, and any assumption of undue finery by a low caste man, meets with instantaneous punishment. Until very lately neither low caste men or women were allowed to wear their cloth or petticoat lower than the knees, whereas the higher castes extend them down to the ground. In the low country of Ceylon, the size and quality of the comb is the great criterion of rank, and if a barber or a shoemaker, or any degraded caste, assumes a comb of extra size and superior quality, he merits exactly the same punishment as he who in the upper country assumes a decent elongation of petticoat.

The feast of the Pirahara attracts great numbers from the surrounding country, and for that reason it was the season fixed upon for the revolt of 1848; but as I before remarked, a premature disturbance in the districts disconcerted the original plans of the rebels. The processions, after parading and annoying the town during eight or ten days, or rather nights, conclude by a grand flare up on the banks of the river Maha-Villaganga, where, amidst a din of pipes and muskets, tomtoms and cracked trumpets, enough to deter the god of rain from ever approaching the spot, if he has any ear for music, a chatty, or large earthen jar, is broken with great solemnity. This ceremony is intended, by some chain of reasoning I must decline explaining, to be typical of copious rain.

I congratulated myself on having been present at this grand Buddhist feast, as it afforded me a very fair opportunity of judging of the beauty of the Kandian ladies, of whose personal attractions I had heard rather fascinating relations. I must confess, the reality woefully disappointed me: neither features nor figures are pleasing, the former being coarse and vulgar, the latter very plump and inelegant: their conceit is most amusing; and the wriggling gait they assume is made doubly ridiculous by the excessive tightness of their *comboys* or petticoats, which confine the free movements of their hips almost as completely as tight straps do, or did (for perhaps the fashion has changed), the shoulders of our fashionable ladies in England. Although this description of plainness is very general in its application, there were some few young ladies who really were not hideous, and who, but for their beastly and universal habit of chewing betel, would have been quite tolerable. The women appear to be even more inveterate chewers than the men; they literally pass their time "twixt betel and chunam," and carry the roll of betel leaves and their little silver or bronze box of chunam or prepared lime, much as a lady does her kerchief or reticule in England. Their method of forming a quid is to place a small piece of lime and Areca nut in a leaf of betel, and roll them up into the shape and size of a large walnut. This is inserted in the cheek, and an active masticatory process commenced, which never ceases, but for the act of expectoration, till all the flavour of the mixture is consumed. The lime acting upon the Areca nut stains the saliva a deep red colour, almost like blood, and imparts to the lips, teeth, and gums, a most filthy and disgusting aspect. The repulsive appearance of the mouth, both in men and women, may account for the fact of their never kissing; this innocent diversion is unknown in Ceylon, to the natives at least. A lover meeting his mistress applies his nose to her cheek, and gives a snuff or a rub, much in the Laputan style of salutation. So utterly disgusting do I hold this betel-chewing propensity, that if Venus φιλομειδής, the laughter-loving goddess herself, decked with the most bewitching of her wreathed smiles, were to appear with betel-stained lips, I really doubt whether the most impassioned of her admirers would not experience some slight disgust.

Polyandry, or the fashion of a lady having several husbands, still maintains, in fact may be said to be almost universal, in the Kandian provinces, and the good-natured wife of Bath, who

> "Husbands at church door, had she had five,
> Withouten other company in youth,"

was quite moderate in her capacity for matrimonial alliance, compared with some of the Kandian fairs. A young lady who espouses one of three brothers becomes as a matter of course the wife of the other two. With our exclusive notions we should find it difficult to reconcile this system with any great amount of domestic comfort; in fact, I think if a full-blooded Englishman, "raised" on beef and porter, were to return home after a day's hunting or shooting, having had *bad* sport, or something else, to put the little black dog on his shoulders, and found two or three fellow husbands, who perhaps would not wait for him to share his evening meal, the intercourse would not be the most cordial or sociable imaginable. However, this system, strange and unnatural as it may appear at first sight, is nevertheless defended by Montesquieu, in an argument that, though jocular, has yet a great deal of reason in it, as being more defensible than polygamy: I cannot say which would be the most popular institution amongst ladies, but I think I can answer for the gentlemen.

It has obtained in Ceylon, from an indisposition in brothers to partition their paternal estate, which must have been the case had they each taken different wives. As it is now, no division of property is necessary: five brothers, the sons possibly of five fathers or uncles and one mother or aunt, marry one wife, and leave their ancestral cocoa-nut or paddy fields entire to their sons and nephews, who again do likewise. This amicable arrangement is not always confined to brothers, although almost universal with them; but a lady who has entered the holy state may add to her stock of spouses, and thus accumulate wealth for her children.

It is remarkable to perceive a rude unpolished nation having recourse to these absurd, exceptional means for preserving an entail, whilst civilized France has resorted to the most stringent regulations for the very opposite purpose. It is the same all over the world—now you see a man hustling to obtain what another is using the same exertion to avoid: here a nation is spending its treasure and blood to overthrow a form of government, or a system of theology, which, in a neighbouring country, would draw the same amount of treasure and blood to its support: here a snake is worshipped as a god, there crushed in disgust:—

> "Here the dull ox now breaks the clod,
> Is now a victim, and now Egypt's god."

If this contradictory policy of the several families and individuals of the same species does not fail to be amusing even to ourselves, how much more so would it be to a man removed from the focus of their attraction, who could view them with the cold reasoning eye of a philosopher; no wonder Plato asserted that the Gods made men for their amusement. The system of Polyandry has necessarily entailed a considerable amount of immorality amongst the female part of the community, and the principle of Comus, that—

> "Beauty is Nature's coin; must not be hoarded,
> But must be current,"

seems to meet with their entire support and patronage. "La belle dame sans merci," celebrated by Alaric Chartien in the days of Charles the Wise, would be a greater object of wonder in the

Ceylon of this, than she could possibly have been in the France of that day.

There is another custom, which the lessened demand for women has introduced, viz. the destruction of female children, which till within a very short period was a maternal right, fully recognised, and very generally practised: there is no doubt that the practice prevails at present, though it is now considered advisable to conceal it. It is a well-known fact in human statistics, that the male births exceed the female; but that in consequence of the loss of life attendant on exposure, excess of food, or other dangers, the number of adult females in all countries exceeds that of men, by, I think, three or four per cent. In Ceylon, however, in a population of some 8 or 900,000, the males exceed the females by some thousands; and so lately as 1821, the population of one district was as fifty-five women to a hundred men. This fact at once proves that female infanticide still exists. The method of destroying the blessed babe, as practised amongst the Buddhists in Ceylon, is very simple; and in a country like England, where infanticide, and the sudden and mysterious removal of husbands, are customs of such frequent occurrence, it is almost surprising that it has not been there introduced. The affectionate mamma puts a few grains of rice in the husk into the infant's throat, and death quickly ensues, without leaving any suspicious appearances.

One naturally feels disgust and horror at national cruelties, such as infanticide and thuggism; but we are apt to forget the beam in our national eye, and to view the mote in that of other countries, as though we occupied a moral height in that respect, from whence we could with self-gratulation consider the backslidings of others; but though we overlook our own little weaknesses, those we condemn do not, and often when the Brahmin is accused of cruelty to his wife or children, and spoken to about national crimes, he answers, "Yes, it is very true, but we do not kill our children, or poison our wives and husbands, for a few rupees, as *in England!*"

In considering the Buddhist's religion, it is very natural to be reminded of the various traditions about our first father, connected with the island of Ceylon: they are numerous and amusing, though to whom the allusions really apply it is difficult to say, whether to Guatama himself, or to some more ancient saint; but certain is it, that throughout the East a very general idea obtained, that Ceylon was the original paradise, and that from thence sprang the race of men: Adam's Bridge, Adam's Footsteps, Adam's Peak, are all objects of veneration and pilgrimage.

However, authorities differ as to the exact part Ceylon had to play in those early days. Some maintain that it was paradise itself, and that on mother Eve's "unfortunate little affair with the Serpent," and the consequent disgrace of herself and her husband, the angel made the bridge of Rocks, traversing the gulf of Manaar, and almost uniting Ceylon with India, to enable them to cross dry footed. Others again maintain that paradise was in the skies, and that Adam and Eve being ejected very hastily by the archangel, and launched on their own resources in the world of space, illustrated the universal law of gravitation, and fell to the ground—Adam alighting on the peak that bears his name, where as a penance he was condemned to stand on one leg for an unlimited number of years, which accounts for only one footstep being visible; Eve fell at Jiddeh, near Mecca, which will explain the very small estimation in which women are held by the Mussulmans. After wandering in search of each other for a hundred years, they at length met on the mountains of Arafat, near Mecca. Adam is described by the legend as a remarkably fine man, upwards of sixty feet high, (the height of the Houris of paradise), with a very handsome face. Which is the correct version I cannot take upon myself to decide, and as in the difficulty which the little boy found in distinguishing Pharaoh from his host, in the peep-show, people of an inquiring turn of mind must follow the very sensible advice of the showman, *and select just which they please.* There is no doubt that if the serpent had any hand in banishing our first parents from their Island Paradise, his seed has rejoiced and gloried in his triumph ever since.

Uniting the two undeniable facts, that Ceylon possesses more snakes and less agricultûral knowledge than any other part of the world, one might almost be led to imagine that Triptolemus, when he had finished his tour of agrarian instruction, turned his team of flying serpents loose in Ceylon, but omitted to leave with them at the same time any knowledge of his art.

CHAPTER VIII.

SNAKES—MUSIC—CEYLON RIFLES—RUNNING A MUCK—COSTUME.

Ceylon is called the Mother of Elephants; it might with equal truth be termed the mamma of snakes; it is a land of snakes, and their numbers seem much greater in the immediate neighbourhood of civilization. I suppose, as in many other cases, particularly in the newly-settled parts of America, it is discovered that man's proximity is not nearly so destructive to certain kinds of game, as is that of their natural enemies. Where foxes and wolves are driven back, the prairie fowl and the deer increase rapidly, in spite of man's most destructive efforts. I fancy that, in Ceylon, the snake finds near the habitations of men an immunity from hawks, pigs, peacocks, mangeese, and their other sharp-sighted and incessant persecutors.

Although death from snake-bites are of rare occurrence, they are yet more frequent in Ceylon than in any other part of the world I have ever visited; two or three deaths occurred in Colombo amongst the natives, during the short time I was there, and several were bitten. In the governor's garden, at Kandy, I have myself killed several tic polongas, merely when strolling through; and the rat-snake, and a beautiful one called the "eye-snake," are so frequently encountered, as to attract little notice.

The eye-snake, so called from a supposed habit it has of striking cattle in the eye when grazing, is without exception the most beautiful and least repulsive of all snakes. It is about four feet long, of the brightest grass green,—the intense green of an English meadow in early summer. It is very thin, and graceful in its movements, and although very rapid when moving, is so instantaneously rigid when alarmed, and adapts itself so wonderfully to the shape and hue of the grass or reeds amongst which it moves, that although watching one intently at your very feet, it is most difficult to discriminate between it and the vegetation with which it mingles. One day, walking at Kandy, I saw what I thought was a large reed, or grass of a most beautiful colour, standing erect on the road some two or three feet from the bank, and it was not till I could have touched it with my hand, that I saw it was an eye-snake coiled up in the road, its head and neck raised about twelve inches from the ground, and as rigid and immovable as if formed of malachite. I possess, I believe, in common with most other persons an irrepressible repugnance to snakes, and have never, that I am aware of, spared any that fell into my power; the eye-snake is the only one I have ever felt any remorse in destroying. It is curious that where snakes are so numerous and so deadly, more deaths do not ensue from them, and that more fear is not displayed by the natives or by settlers. After seeing a cobra, or tic polonga, glide from the grass almost under your feet, you feel a "kinder" start, and "walk delicately" for a few minutes, but this feeling very soon quits you, and you rush and push your way through jungle and grass, without any look of dread. Still, however hardened you may become, it *does* require a good amount of practice and self-command not to show any surprise or to start at finding a snake at the toe of your boot, or a scorpion under your pillow. A lady, whose acquaintance I had the pleasure of making in the island, told me that one night, as she turned down the sheets to step into bed, she saw a large cobra coiled up close to the pillow. A snake in the grass is bad enough, but a snake in bed would be doubly disagreeable. I don't know why it is that the horror of a snake should be so universal to men and animals; it does not attack mankind for food; and except in one or two species in South America and the West Indies, flies his presence with the greatest assiduity.

There is something so persevering and unrelenting in the character of the snake, that one can quite understand the reasoning that prompted such nations as the Mexicans, Egyptians, Babylonians, Hindus, and Buddhists, who worship the power of Evil, solely for its power and omnipotence, to treat them as deities. The worship of the snake and the bull, indeed, are two very striking superstitions that in olden days seem to have pervaded the entire world; and it is remarkable that all fables of the creation and early history of the world, in all religions, contain some myth regarding the serpent.

I took a good deal of trouble to inquire the size of the boa-python, as found in Ceylon, but though I heard of several that within the memory or tradition of men had been killed, measuring thirty feet, I never heard that size exceeded; but this by no means proves that their growth is limited to that length, or that they may not exist in large numbers. Game of all kinds is so plentiful in Ceylon, that they need never be forced into the neighbourhood of man to procure their food. In India, I know from eye-witnesses, of their being killed forty-five feet long, and six feet in circumference; and the one killed in the Sunderbund some years ago was credibly reported at sixty feet: moreover, in proof that this need not be an exaggeration, we may remember that the snake that stopped the army of Attilius Regulus in the river Bagrada, was 120 feet, and that its skeleton was preserved in Rome till within some three or four centuries.

Ceylon is certainly a grand place for the study of ophiology, and the varieties are more numerous than charming. It is curious that, although every one of the four orders of Reptilia are represented in each hemisphere, not one appears in exactly the same form; the serpents, alligators, batrachians, and chelonians of either hemisphere, though excessively similar, are not identical. All this must be a source of great interest and delight to the naturalist, but to the traveller it is not always a cause of so much satisfaction. It may not be uninteresting to name a few of the varieties, and their peculiarities, as stated by competent authority. Omitting all such as are oviparous, and are innocuous, except from their strength, I will mention those that are ovoviviparous and poisonous. Of cobras or hooded snakes there are four kinds,—the *Cobra di Capello*, or *serpent à lunettes*, esteemed sacred by the Buddhist, and looked upon as the emblem of wisdom, but still slain on all occasions; the *Cobra Minalle*, with whose peculiarities I am not acquainted; the *Cobra di Morte*, a delightful variety, of some six or nine inches in length, with a skull and cross-bones marked on the head!! (I give the story as it was told to me, but it is only fair to say, I don't believe it); its bite is almost instantaneously fatal: the *Cobra Aurelia*, about six inches long, that displays a predilection for crawling into person's ears, and causing death by frenzy, (*vide* "Hamlet.") Of these four species, I can only speak from experience of the cobra di capello, never having seen any individual of the other three. The Minny Polonga, or *Tic Polonga*, are the most common in the Kandian country: they are very quick and lively in their movements, and their bite is not attended with the fearful agony that generally accompanies snake venom. The bite is succeeded by a lethargic apathy, very much like that induced by laudanum, and the only chance of saving the patient is to keep him moving, for if once allowed to sleep, it is the sleep of death, that knows no waking.

Of all snakes the cobra is the most beautiful, and when erect, with its hood expanded, gracefully moving in time to the music, it is certainly a most striking and fascinating object; its eye, which is in general leaden and heavy, becomes, under the influence of music, intensely bright and glittering. This effect is heightened by the fact of snakes having no eyelids; the eye, although so beautiful, is not strong, and cannot bear any strong glare; this was well known to the ancients, who had an idea that the flash of an emerald deprived them of sight. The poison from the fang of a cobra is like one or two drops of laudanum. It is said, and I believe with truth, that it loses a joint of its tail every time it expends its poison. The cobra is *par excellence* the sacred snake amongst Hindoos and Buddhists, and with the latter has attained that enviable position from a myth of its having with its hood shaded Buddha, when sleeping, from the sun. It must have been a "pretty considerable tall snake that, and no mistake." The Cingalese believe that there is a world full of cobras, whose forms are tenanted by the souls of men, who, in life, had been free from every vice but malice: they are Buddhists in faith, worship in temples, reside in furnished houses, and enjoy society, living on the best of "chicken fixings,"—they may, in fact, have any variety of food they can desire, with this peculiarity, that it must always assume the form of a frog. They have a king, who is the biggest; and they retain the distinctions of high and low caste; the light-coloured snakes constituting the former, the darker ones, the latter. I cannot imagine what there is so enticing in the existence or habits of snakes, that should have induced people in all ages to covet their form in a future state? Cadmus and his wife, after having, by-the-bye, had a good deal to do with dragons and snakes in their life-time, were by choice converted into snakes; and the pet boy of one of the mission-schools at Kandy, being asked by a visitor what he hoped to become in a future state, answered, "A cobra." The delight of living in a land free from snakes and other noxious insects, is a blessing which we do not appreciate till we have experienced the horror and annoyance of the contrary.

There is a large detachment of Ceylon Rifles constantly stationed at Kandy; and these, with a wing of some Queen's regiment, form a very respectable force. The Rifles were originally recruited entirely by Malays from the eastern islands, the recruiting head-quarters being at Singapore; but, for some reason, the service has within the last few years become unpopular, and few can be persuaded to join. The only Malays, therefore, that now join the ranks are youngsters born and bred in the regiment itself. The vacancies have lately been filled up chiefly by Kaffirs; they are a more powerful race, and not so revengeful as the Malays, but are rather given to "look too often at their little fingers,"—as the language of slang, so constantly used by the male, and tolerated, to say the least of it, by the female portion of society in these days, expresses the vice of drinking too freely.

The Kaffirs, notwithstanding their thick skulls and unintellectual appearance, have a very remarkable turn for music, and seven-eighths at least of the Rifle band keep time to the dulcet tones, with blubber lips, woolly heads, and heels of African elongation. A belief has commonly prevailed in England, that thin lips are advantageous for good execution on wind instruments, especially the flute and cornet-à-piston; but this theory seems unfounded, for the Kaffir solo-players of the Rifle band, with lips of any imaginary dimensions, both as regards width and thickness, strike the highest notes with as much clearness and precision as any European performer could boast of; they are also excellent timeists.

It appears a fact worthy of the notice of the student of ethnology, that the races, whether human or animal, that inhabit the continent of Africa, have been particularly favoured by nature in the development of their terminations, whether frontal or posterior. The tail of the Cape sheep is famed throughout the world for its size; the "fact" of the Hottentot women far exceeds anything that "fiction" has hitherto ventured to produce amongst the goddesses of our own country; and the heel of a real "Bull Nigger" is almost, if not quite, as long as the fore part of his understanding; the horns, too, of the oxen, and the different varieties of deer, are most remarkable; even the horses have large heads.

The Ceylon Rifles are held in particular dread and abhorrence by the natives; and the latter feeling, without being tempered by any dread whatever, is the reciprocal sentiment of the Rifles, especially the Malays. In 1848, this feeling was illustrated by many, and in some cases bloody, instances. The Rifles are active, dapper men, and well drilled for a field day; but, unfortunately, coming of races used to their own peculiar kind of warfare from childhood, they find it difficult to forget the manners and customs of their fathers, and are rather apt, in the heat of an engagement, to forget their European education, and discarding all the advantages of discipline and mutual dependence, to break their ranks, fling away their muskets, and, trusting entirely to their daggers and kreeses, to rush upon the enemy in their national manner, and work away each man on his own hook. This, of course, answers very well in bush-fighting; but if opposed by discipline, would be utterly fatal. In several instances in the rebellion of 1848, the detachments sent against the Kandians disobeyed the orders of their officers, and, to use an expression especially applied to the Malays, "ran a muck" amongst their opponents. The loss they inflicted on the Kandians is not well ascertained, but there is little doubt that it was severe. It is not in war, however, only that the Malay "runs a muck;" it happens occasionally—happily, not so frequently as formerly—amongst all Malays, and it is an attack they are liable to at all seasons. Every Malay, whether household servant or shopkeeper, or in whatever line of life he may be, carries a kreese concealed about his person: sometimes it is worn in the turban; sometimes on the thigh, in the same manner as a carpenter carries his rule: this is drawn on any insult or paroxysm, and used freely against the persons of all who may come across them.

When a Malay runs a muck, he is animated by much the same feeling as the fanatics of Arabia and the East; he has no idea of saving his own life, and only seeks to destroy as many others as he can, before he is overpowered. A case happened not long ago at Bombay, which will illustrate the expression. A Malay courted a girl, who refused him; he asked a last interview, which was granted. He came, and entered into conversation with her, when, suddenly drawing out a concealed kreese, he stabbed her in six places; and then, (on the principle, I suppose, of the more the merrier,) stabbed five other persons, who were not only totally unconnected with the unfortunate female, but who would willingly have suffered him to depart, had he been so inclined. He gave himself up directly the guard appeared, and was hung. The Kaffirs of the regiment are nearly all Roman Catholics; the Malays, Mussulmans.

I suppose the great object of dressing Asiatics in the inelegant and inconvenient costume of European soldiers, is to destroy the individual energy of the man, and to foster, as much as possible, the European notions of discipline and mutual dependence. It is to be lamented that this desirable consummation cannot be effected with a greater regard to national costume. The Malay, for instance, with his turban placed slightly on one side, like the "Cornu Ducale" of the Genoese Doges, his full easy robe gathered up as high as necessity may require, or flowing down to the heels, render him a much more imposing object, and allow him far greater liberty of limb and action, than the trussed circumstance of the tight jacket, stiff stock, and fatiguing cross-belt of the English fashion. A Malay in the former costume bears as much resemblance to the same animal in the latter, as the plaided and kilted Highlander, swelling with braes and importance, does to the limp choker and tight dress-coat of a tavern waiter.

CHAPTER IX.

CINGALESE COMMERCE—RAJAH WILLAH—CROPS AND CULTIVATION—ELEPHANTS—CINGALESE HOSPITALITY—FOOD IN THE JUNGLE.

THE mercantile history of Ceylon is a very remarkable one, and the undulations of the wave of commercial prosperity have there been more than ordinarily fluctuating. It has alternately been looked upon as a commercial El Dorado, where money was made without either labour or residence, and as an island which no efforts would render remunerative. It is undeniable that it has proved a perfect commercial maelstrom, that has sucked in, and ejected, ruined and swamped, all who sported on its waters. The sum it owes to the commercial and monied community of England and India is enormous; and I doubt whether any spot of similar magnitude, excepting perhaps the Goodwin Sands, has swallowed so much wealth with so much pertinacity, and with so total an absence of all return.

About fifteen years ago, when the price of coffee was exorbitant, the report suddenly pervaded the mercantile and speculative community that that aromatic berry grew and flourished in especial luxuriance in the island of Ceylon. Land was said to be for purchase at almost nominal prices; labour was reported to be plentiful at rather less than nothing; and it was proved by the clearest reasoning and the most undeniable facts, that coffee, then fetching 100*s.* or 120*s.* per cwt., could be grown and offered for sale in the European markets for 30*s.* or 40*s.* per cwt. The land of Ceylon was affirmed to be the most fertile in the world, and the market crop that might be expected was 15 or 20 cwt. an acre; thus showing a clear return of at least 50*l.* or 60*l.* per acre, or 15,000*l.* or 18,000*l.* per annum from an estate of 300 acres. These profits, though so enormous and startling, were yet so plausibly argued, and left so large a margin for deduction, that the most wary were imposed upon, and did not hesitate to invest their all in the business. What was an investment of 30,000*l.* or 40,000*l* for a certain return of 10,000*l.* or 20,000*l.* per annum for ever? It was a second South Sea Bubble; the only difference being, that no roguery was exercised in getting up the cry, and few persons but the native workmen of Ceylon and India gained by the expenditure. These golden visions, though from time to time damped and deferred by the painful experience that land is neither bought nor cleared for nothing, that expenses were erroneously stated, that labour was 6*d.* or 8*d.* a day, and dear at that price, considering the amount of labour performed, were still cherished and kept alive by men who, having involved either all or the greater part of their fortunes, could not reconcile themselves to the notion that they had voluntarily imposed upon themselves and were ruined, and still went on working at a loss, not unfrequently borrowing for that purpose at exorbitant interest, and, as a set-off to their endless expenses, still consoling themselves with the high market price of the bean.

However, the commercial crash of 1846 and 1847 put an end to dreams of wealth, and substituted very clearly-defined visions of exacting creditors, cold-blooded judges, with prisons, bailiffs, and sponging-houses continually flitting in the distance. The fact is, they were ruined. Coffee fell from 90*s.* or 130*s.* to 50*s.* or 70*s.* The money market was straitened; they were compelled to pay off their incumbrances, or to resign themselves to more exorbitant exactions in the shape of interest and premiums. A total bankruptcy overspread the island; scores of estates were abandoned, and those who recovered by sale a fifteenth part of their original venture, were considered fortunate men indeed. Capitalists then on the spot bought for a few hundreds, estates that had cost as many thousands.

The island is now, however, fast recovering from the exhaustion and uncertainty unavoidable from such a feverish state of affairs. The price of coffee has not risen, nor is it likely to do so; but the expenses of clearing, planting, and managing estates have been so far reduced, that to a resident, coffee planting not only offers a fair investment, but is excessively remunerative. With good management, a coffee estate should yield from 7 to 10 cwt. per acre, and should (deducting every expense) clear from 17*s*. to 20*s*. per cwt. This is supposing a case where the soil and climate are both favourable, and carriage and labour not above the average.

About nine miles from Kandy is situated the estate called Rajah Willah, which is, without any exception, I should imagine, the finest in the world. It has been planted some twenty or thirty years, yet the trees are as healthy and vigorous as though only a fourth or fifth of that age. The amount of crop is really astonishing: last year it averaged 27 cwt. per acre, on an estate of 200 acres, and there is little doubt but that with the increased and increasing science of coffee planting, and the economising of labour, its production will not only increase, but will be still more remunerative.

The advantages of manure have been especially

developed in coffee culture, for not only is it proved that the crop is increased thereby even to the extent of one-third, but it is ascertained beyond a doubt that in districts where the coffee shrub was liable to frequent injury, if not total destruction, from continued droughts, the application of manure has not only increased the general production, but has answered the purpose of constant and organized irrigation. Rajah Willah, when I visited it, had been suffering from a severe drought of five or six months, and it was very remarkable that those portions of the estate that were unmanured, were parched and shrunk, whilst those that had been dressed, displayed the most perfect verdure and healthiness.

It is not necessary to travel much in Ceylon, to be struck by glaring and constant instances of too sanguine speculations attended with complete and utter ruin. Not two miles from Kandy, you pass a sugar estate, and ranges of boiling houses, &c. &c.; the latter are in a dilapidated, almost ruinous condition; and it is evident, from the scrubby appearance of the cane and the smallness of its produce, that the expectations of the owner when he erected the works, were founded on calculations of a return which have never been realized. During the days when every undertaking in Ceylon was supposed to be golden in its results, it was assumed as a matter of course that sugar would grow and be remunerative in any part of Ceylon; but such is far from being the case; the soil is unsuited to its growth, the climate far from favourable, and the immediate neighbourhood of Madras—where labour is one-tenth at least of the expense, and the soil and climate unexceptionable—will always compel the planters of Ceylon to enter the lists under disadvantages, which it will require constant progress and the scientific application of unlimited capital to overcome. The soil in parts of the Madras presidency is, indeed, so suitable for sugar, labour so cheap, and means of shipment so easy, that there is little doubt but that if things go on as they are now doing, a considerable proportion of the world's consumption will be derived from thence. I heard an account of a sugar estate in Madras, from the manager himself, the labour on which was inconceivably low. The average wages of 500 men, including clerks, blacksmiths, coopers, &c., was six shillings a-month!! The highest *refined* sugar could be shipped for 7*l.* per ton. In the Havannah, 8*l.* per ton for *unrefined* sugar is considered low.

As one advances up the country, the instances of abandoned or weed-ridden estates increase at every step, and throughout the entire distance from Kandy to Kotmalie, thirty or five and thirty miles, the country, though formerly to a considerable extent under cultivation, does not now display one single instance of a thriving and remunerative estate.

About four miles from Kandy, the road to Newera Elia, Kotmalie, Badula and the east coast, crosses the river Mahavilla Ganga.* The river at that point is straight, deep, and broad, and presents a very noble appearance. The bridge is one of the most graceful of the kind I have ever seen; it is one single span, of two hundred and seven feet, and is composed entirely of Satinwood; it was built by Sir Edward Barnes, as a completion to the magnificent road from Colombo to Kandy. The Kandians held a sort of superstition, that when their mountain was pierced, and their river bridged, all hope of defending their country would be at an end. Sir Edward Barnes, with a laudable desire of fulfilling this prophecy, and, like Semiramis, Decebalus, Abimelech, or Macduff, wishing to avail himself of the aid of superstition to strike terror into his enemies, made a small tunnel through a portion of the rock, and constructing the bridge, quite convinced the Kandians that their day was

* Or, Sandy River, from the arenaceous nature of its bed.

come, and that all chance of opposing their destiny, or of liberating themselves, was hopeless.*

We proceeded the first twelve miles along the Kotmalie road, in a stage, and a very indifferent one too. It was preferable to walking, and that was all that could be said in its favour. The road was exceedingly pretty, and the brilliant green of the paddy-fields, raised in broad irregular steps one above the other, and taking advantage of any little streams to stretch away far up into the jungle, had a very pleasing effect.

At this village we stayed for the night, intending to ride on twenty-seven miles, to Kotmalie, in the morning. The fleas, the Pariah dogs, and a sweet infant, who, although not my bedfellow, was only separated from me by the most fragile of bulkheads, rendered the night's rest anything but satisfactory. The fleas seemed to move in measure to the yells of the infant and the snarling of the curs; and when 4 A.M. had arrived, I was only too delighted to jump up, and cry, "To horse!" Unfortunately, however, for my feverish haste,

* Abimelech, when besieging the tower of Shechem, made each of his soldiers carry a branch, to conceal their numbers, and strike a superstitious dread into his enemies. Semiramis stuffed bullock-skins, and placed them on camels, to resemble elephants. Decebalus, in the first century, deceived the warlike Romans by causing a forest to be felled in a single night, and armour to be stuck on the stumps of the trees. Macduff's little ruse was probably taken from Abimelech.

which I intended to soothe with a rattling gallop, one of the steeds had not arrived, and Punchy was the only quadruped that appeared at my reiterated summons. My companion was some thirteen stone, and myself about ten, and although Punchy was doubtless strong enough to bear the combined weight of twenty-three stone, his back was remarkably short and broad, and we should have found considerable difficulty in locating ourselves upon it, especially as the ingenious animal had an interesting habit of depressing and elevating his extremities in a most sudden and unexpected manner. Consequently, we set out to walk, hoping every mile to meet the horse. We had an agreeable walk of twelve miles to a village (I will not attempt the Cingalese names, since most of them are *unspellable, unpronounceable,* and take up considerable space), where we breakfasted. The road was more picturesque than the day before—the mountains assuming grander forms, and the foliage becoming less tropical in its appearance; throughout the journey, the character of the scenery underwent a complete change every ten minutes. At one moment it would remind us of Devonshire, and the Isle of Wight; now of the chalk hills of Surrey and Sussex, and then again of the softer beauties of Tweedside, with its rapid roaring river flashing in the morning sun. It was a delicious walk, and the sun by no means oppressive.

We passed an elephant working on the road; and it was most interesting to watch the half-reasoning brute; he was tearing out large roots from the ground by means of a chain and hook, fastened round his neck with a species of collar. He pulled like a man, or rather like a number of men, with a succession of steady hauls, throwing his whole weight into it, and almost going down on his knees, turning round every now and then to see what progress he was making. Really the instinct displayed by the elephant in its domesticated state, is little short of reason in its fullest sense. There is no doubt they do think, and also act upon experience and memory, and their capacity seems to increase in an extraordinary degree from their intercourse with man. The remarkable nicety and trouble they take in squaring and arranging the blocks of hewn stone when building a bridge is incredible, unless seen; they place them with as much skill as any mason, and will return two or three times to give the finishing touches when they think the work is not quite perfect. They retire a few yards and consider what they have effected, and you almost fancy you can detect them turning their sagacious old noddles on one side, and shutting one eye in a knowing manner, to detect any irregularity in the arrangement. Sidney Smith's anecdotes of elephants' reason in his Lectures on Moral Philosophy, although most astonishing, do not fail for the want of corroboration. I heard numerous anecdotes almost as extraordinary as those he mentions; and amongst others, one of an elephant at Tinnevelly that had been engaged all day in piling logs of timber, but in the evening, becoming angry at some promise his keeper had neglected to fulfil, he went of his own accord and undid every stroke of work he had completed during the day. The exact line of demarcation between instinct and reason, although so frequently and ably discussed, is still left an open question, as it always must be. Great admiration has lately been excited in London and Paris by the remarkable agility of elephants which stand on their heads and perform other gymnastic feats; but, wonderful as they are, they are nothing new in the annals of elephantine activity, and, in fact, compared with some of the relations of former days, they sink into insignificance. Pliny (but he is rather a mendacious authority) mentions having seen four dance on a tight rope, and nurse another pretending to be sick; but Dion, Suetonius, Seneca, and Plutarch, more credible authorities, each mention their tight-rope capabilities.

After breakfast we progressed again, and here took place one of those ridiculous little traits of obstinacy, of which only Englishmen could be guilty There being only one steed, neither would be the first to acknowledge any fatigue, but each kindly urged the other to mount, and declared himself to be as fresh as paint; the consequence was, we trudged on with Punchy's fat little carcase jogging after us. We found our walk was a good twenty-seven miles up hill, and were by no means sorry to fetch our haven under the hospitable roof of a coffee-planter. A walk of this distance immediately on landing from ship-board, and in the tropics, was a little too severe, and rather a dangerous experiment.

Some, or rather many of the Bungalows on the coffee estates are most agreeably situated, with very fine views; they are built without any very great expense, and contain a considerable amount of comfort. Hospitality is genuine and unrestricted among the planters in Ceylon; you ride up to a Bungalow, put your horse into the stable, enter the house, and if the owner be at home introduce yourself, or if you have a companion introduce him, and he performs the same kind office for you; if the owner is not in, you nevertheless introduce yourself to his butler, as the housekeepers are called, light a cheroot, call for beer, &c., and make yourself at home till his return. The conversation on entering a planter's Bungalow, whether friend or not, is usually on this wise:—"Master at home?" "No, sar." "Beer got?" "Yes, sar." "Beer bring. Cheroot got?" "Yes, sar." "Now then, you nigger, bring a light, and get something to eat." "Yes, sar." This free and easy way of proceeding is expected and universally practised. It is a sort of communism of the pleasantest description, and is necessitated by the state and extent of the population; for where Bungalows are twelve and twenty miles apart, roads barely passable, and weather during six months of the year inclement, the wonted ceremonious and formal introductions of more civilized society would be out of place, and highly disagreeable to the hungry, moistened voyager.

The food in the jungle is not always of the most delicate and tempting nature; it is chiefly gallinaceous; roast chicken and egg-curry, or fried egg and chicken-curry, form the chief staples of a planter's subsistence. A great jungle dish is a chicken ravished from the roost, killed, and immediately split open and gutted; it is with great propriety called a de-spatch cock; and it is extraordinary how by this summary conjunction of the culinary and executionary art, the most fibrous and indigestible of cocks can be converted into the most delicious and tender of chickens.

Beef is certainly to be had occasionally, as is also mutton, but the difficulty is to eat it when procured; as is invariably the case in warm climates, the meat has neither the flavour nor succulence of that of more temperate regions.

CHAPTER X.

COFFEE PLANTATIONS—RAILROADS—THE TAMULS—THEIR DISLIKE OF THE CINGALESE.

THE coffee shrub, as everybody knows, or as everybody can know, who will take the trouble of visiting Kew or Chiswick, is very regular and ornamental in its growth and shape. When well trained and pruned, it resembles a miniature tree, rather than a shrub. In Ceylon it is planted six or seven feet apart, in rows about five feet distant from each other; and the ground selected as most advantageous to the growth and training of the shrub lies, with scarcely any exception, on the face of the mountain side, often very precipitous.

When seen from a distant point of view, two or three hundred acres planted with coffee do not improve the landscape, giving it rather a scrubby appearance; but, as you approach nearer, and are able to distinguish the blossom on the trees, and the coffee-berries "fit for plucking," the contrast of the white flower on the dark green leaves, and the red berries clustering in masses, has a very pleasing effect.

It has been discovered that those districts that formerly produced the finest forest, now yield the finest coffee; and, in consequence, several of them have been bought up, and speculation is still rife, and *hard at work*.

The life of a coffee-planter is monotonous to a degree, and to any one without very considerable powers of solitary intellectual enjoyment, would be little short of unbearable. During the crop season, from the middle of October or beginning of November to the end of February, he can indeed find constant employment for eyes and ears, in watching and listening to the monotonous rattle of the pulpers, as they divest the coffee-berry of its scarlet overcoat; but this is a kind of occupation that would surfeit the most patient in a few days; there is not the slightest interest in it; and if his mind is engaged at all, it must be with objects outside the pulping-house, rather than with those within. The manager or owner on his estate in crop season is in this position; he cannot accelerate the work much by his presence, but he knows that if he is absent, the business will be retarded. During the other months of the year, hoeing and weeding, thinking of dinner, and wondering whether the bug will visit him, or whether he will ever be clear from its present attack, form the chief employment and most interesting speculation of the coffee-planter in the jungle. There are no interesting current subjects of conversation in the island: the planter soon loses all interest in European matters, and he finds nothing to supply the blank. A musician might find occupation in the exercise of his art, an intellectual man in the cultivation of his mind; but the musician, without the pleasure of sharing or imparting his enthusiasm to others, and the intellectual man, without the alembic of society, and the wholesome friction with other minds, will find the pursuit of pleasure under such difficulties irksome and monotonous, and very likely to end in disappointment and disgust.

The coffee-planter has not the diversified occupation of the English farmer, who finds such continual interest in the variety and rotation of the objects of his culture, and in the price and improved breeds of stock, &c.; he has but one crop, which never varies, except in the amount of its yield, or in the presence or absence of its great enemy, the bug

This scourge of the coffee plantations resembles the cochineal insect of Madeira; its effects are very varied, and the time for which it attaches itself to estates is indefinite. It will occasionally disappear entirely after a visit of two years, and the proprietor may be congratulating himself on a prospective good crop, and perhaps runs down to Colombo for a fortnight's lark on the strength of it, when, on his return, he finds that his enemy is there before him, as bad, if not worse, than ever. The leaves become perfectly black, and encrusted with a soot-like substance, much like laurels growing in the smoke of London; they do not fall off, neither are they injured; for, after the bug disappears, they come out greener and fresher than ever, but the fruit withers under its devastating effects before arriving at maturity, and a crop of ten cwt. per acre will dwindle to two or three.

Improve his shrubs the planter can, by careful cultivation and manure, but still that improvement is very limited, and its progress very tardy; any attempt to keep stock for the formation of manure is the pursuit of pleasure under very great difficulties; for the dampness of the mountains is quite unsuited to oxen; and even pigs—the hardiest of all animals, and the only one, except man, that can flourish in any climate from the Equator to the Pole—die in great numbers.

When the railroads are finished, and carriage from Colombo becomes much cheaper, there is little doubt that artificial manure will come into play, and cause a considerable increase in the yield of the island.

The total production of coffee is now about one-fourth of that of Java, one-eighth of that of the Brazils. It is doubted whether Java can greatly increase her production, though little doubt is entertained that the Brazils can do so largely: oppressive export duties still trammel and debar the free course of her commerce, but they are being gradually relaxed, a proceeding which cannot fail to increase her trade most materially. Already railroads have been commenced; and abolition of slavery, instead of paralyzing the planters and merchants, as was anticipated, seems to have impressed them with the necessity of increased activity, and instilled into them a considerable amount of the leaven of American and English energy, which before was quite unknown. Ceylon has the misfortune of being a colony, or rather a conquered country, and its dependence on the governing power some 15,000 miles off, checks and enfeebles its individual energies and exertions.

A railroad has been talked of, discussed, planned, and sanctioned in Ceylon: but somehow, although not more than a month is consumed in the transit of the 15,000 miles, delay after delay has sprung up, and there is now exactly the same chance of its being completed as there was two years ago. Its enormous importance to the planter, in importing rice and manure from the coast at a cheap rate, and in exporting coffee, cannot be too highly estimated; the natural difficulties of the country are not very great, and if the constructors will proceed on the economical and practical principles that have been adopted in America, and which should have been brought into play in India, there is little doubt that two years might see it completed; if, on the other hand, they follow out the extravagant ideas on which railroads are formed in England, it is much to be feared that their capital and ardour will be exhausted long before the rail is half completed.

In all cases where the energetic "*few*" wish to persuade the apathetic "many" to any undertaking obviously for their benefit, it is politic, and even necessary, to take advantage of any temporary reaction or impulse that may arise, either from hope of immediate profit, or from any kind of *esprit de corps*. "Hope deferred" not only sickens, but it destroys all energy, and generally ends in apathy and *insouciance*. This is especially the case where different interests are concerned: a mixed community is seldom constant or stable for any length of time, and is easily diverted from its purpose, unless kept well up to the mark. In Ceylon, the majority, eager and desirous for the railroad three years ago, have during that time gradually diminished in ardour and exertion; and whilst, owing to their own apathy, they are unable to advance one single fresh argument in its favour, the minority are enabled to assume a higher position, and appeal to experience for their former opinion of its impossibility.

Coffee estates vary from one to three hundred acres—and produce from five to ten cwt. an acre; their profits vary with the prevailing price of coffee in Europe, and of labour, and the inscrutable effects of the season; but from 15*s.* to 20*s.* net profit per cwt. may be considered a high average; any yield under five cwt. per acre scarcely pays its expenses; any over seven cwt. pays handsomely.

All the roads are very perpendicular, many excessively dangerous; and it is said, the fact of the planters constantly riding up hill, accounts for their round shoulders, and certainly four out of five have that peculiarity.

Although the scenery is magnificent, the riding in Ceylon is most disagreeable. You seldom can go out of a slow canter, and more usually, unless you are quite reckless of consequences, you are inclined to walk.

All the labour on a coffee estate is performed by coolies from the Malabar coast; they are chiefly Tamuls, but amongst them are some Mahrattas from Kandeish. They are a docile, inoffensive race, and when well treated, they contract a certain cat-like affection for their masters, and for particular localities. On several estates there are numbers that have been born and bred, and will probably be buried there. A coolie, after working hard for a month, and deducting every expense for his rice and house, can earn from 12*s.* to 14*s.*, which for them is very good. The habit of the greater number is, to come over for the coffee harvest, as the Irish do for the grain harvest in England, and to starve, and almost deprive themselves of the necessaries of life, whilst in the island, that they may take back as much as they can, to squander or support them in idleness for the next few months.

The Tamuls are not good hands at hard labour, such as hewing or digging; and in these two matters the Cingalese, when working on contract, beat them easily; but they are very apt to acquire all the horticultural knowledge necessary for pruning, topping, &c., and in hoeing and picking coffee they, and especially the women, perform as good service as the most muscular race in the world. They are located in long sheds, called lines, and may work or not, as they choose, no compulsion being allowed; of course, receiving no pay for those days they remain idle.

They have no partiality whatever for the Cingalese; and if the rebellion of 1848 had come to a head, I have no doubt they would have protected their masters and their property to the best of their power. One instance occurred, which showed this disposition in a strong light. The owner of an estate was absent from home, when his manager, a Malabar native, heard that some hundreds of Cingalese were approaching the bungalow to steal and to ravish; he had not much time to procure assistance, and had to trust entirely to his own resources. He immediately dressed up some fifteen or twenty coolies in his master's European attire, and placed them in the verandah on chairs and tables, in a *dégagé* kind of manner, concealing their black physogs as much as possible with straw hats, &c. The Cingalese, approaching with caution to reconnoitre, were startled by seeing such a number of what they took for Europeans, and, being seized with a panic, fled precipitately, supposing the intended victims had been made aware of their intention, and assembled a party of friends for the purpose of giving them a warmer reception than they desired.

CHAPTER XI.

"PUNCHY"—START FOR NEWERA ELIA—LEECHES—STOPPED AT A RIVER—SCENERY—ARRIVE AT NEWERA ELIA.

AFTER enjoying the kind hospitality of the planters of Kotmalie for some five or six days, we completed our arrangement for our further progress to Newera Elia and Badula.

During these few days, I had the pleasure of increasing my acquaintance with "Punchy," my pony. I found the change of climate had effected no alteration in his mischievous disposition; his antics and tricks were as continual as ever; but little peculiarities of curvetting, or standing on his tail or head, which in the broad flat roads of the low country were only annoying or ridiculous, were, in the narrow precipitous paths of the mountains, actually dangerous. Several times, in his reckless attempts at a lark, he got his hind legs over precipices of most unpleasant abruptness; once, indeed, he was more than half over, and but that the soil was fortunately firm, we must have rolled a distance of some hundred feet. He had a very disagreeable propensity also of trying to bolt into stables, kitchens, or, in fact, any outhouses with low doorways, that came in his way; and being remarkably small himself, he did not apparently consider the additional height of his rider. I should have parted with him, but he was so strong and hardy, that I trusted to long journeys and short rations to bring him to his proper bearings.

C—— had invested in a quadruped which was the very opposite of mine in every respect. If the goddess of mischief and god of pleasantry had presided at the accouchement of my pony's parent, the deities of sloth and patience must have taken an active part in presiding at that of C——'s. If the term "patient in long suffering" can be applied to an animal, he certainly possessed it in an eminent degree. No amount or intensity of kicks, blows, or abuse had the slightest effect in accelerating his movements; his vitality, instead of being diffused generally over his whole body, seemed to be confined to particular parts, and his sense of feeling to be composed of a number of "senses of feeling" entirely unconnected with each other. No one blow had any visible effect but on the part actually struck; a blow on the head, for instance, or the hind quarters, would turn the head slightly, and cause a wincing in the quarter struck, but it would not in the slightest degree have the effect of increasing his speed; the only means of effecting that was to strike all the several seats of feeling one after another as quickly as possible, and by that means a sort of combination of power was acquired, which caused a momentary acceleration of speed. The pony was formed on most remarkable lines of equestrian architecture: his fore and hind quarters appeared to have no connexion with each other whatever. The fore quarters were always either pulling forward the hind, or being pushed forward by them; they never moved in unison, or with any appearance of being impelled by the same equine will.

Our companion had procured volunteers amongst the coolies of the adjoining estate for our party, and on the 6th July they were despatched, to the number of forty, with tents, edibles, potables, physic, guns, and ammunition, to Badula, a distance of some seventy-five or eighty miles; they would probably take four or five days to accomplish that journey, whereas we intended to ride it in two. We ourselves started before daybreak on the 8th, intending to reach Newera Elia that evening, and progressed very satisfactorily for the first eight miles, the roads bad, but passable.

Our route for a considerable distance lay through patna, or open grass lands, and the number of leeches that there attacked us and the horses was perfectly incredible; they were hanging on the horses' fetlocks and on the horse-keeper's legs in bunches, and even on horseback as we were, and only occasionally brushed by the long grass, they managed to board us, and the first intimation one had of their presence was a sensation of some cold heavy body hanging to one's flesh. They are excessively small when lean, and can insert their disgusting bodies through the smallest crevices, but they swell in an extraordinary manner, and when replete and gorged, are almost as large as a European leech in that state.

Their quickness of vision and the celerity of their hoop-like progress is very remarkable. When you stop in a patna, although there may not be a leech visible, in less than a minute you will see them hurrying, thin and hungry, from all quarters. They are most undaunted in their attacks, and most adhesive in their attentions. They illustrate the expression of sticking to one like a leech, more than any other kind I have seen. It is sometimes impossible to detach them, and you are obliged to squeeze them to death in the position they occupy, by no means an agreeable alternative. Their bite is excessively poisonous, and you frequently see scars and sores on the natives' understandings, arising solely from that cause. The wound is succeeded by intense itching, and the unwary griff who scratches will assuredly suffer. The larger kind of leech used for medicinal purposes is also found in numbers in Ceylon, but I am not aware that they are exported. The smaller kind that I have been describing, attack the cattle when grazing, and effectually prevent their improving or acquiring flesh when feeding on patna. I do not know that they are found in any other part of the world but Ceylon and the western ghauts of India.

The rains had been very heavy during the past few days, and doubts had been expressed by competent authority as to the chance of our being stopped at a river it was necessary to swim *en route* to Newera Elia; however, as the river had only been impassable once or twice before within the memory of any one there, we had trusted to chance, and had omitted sending anybody forward to ascertain its condition. We were horribly disgusted, therefore, after a ride of ten miles, to find ourselves on the brink of a river nearly as broad as the Thames at Hampton, rushing along, foaming and impetuous, at a speed and with a depth of stream that forbade any idea of our being able to cross our horses. The ferry-boat, indeed, which consisted of two canoes, fastened together at a distance of about two feet, and which no force of waves or current could have capsized, might cross by ascending the stream in the back current for some hundreds of yards above the landing-place, descending in the middle of the stream like an arrow, till it struck the back current on the other side some distance below, and again ascended to the landing-place. These back currents were caused by a wall of rocks some hundred yards below the landing-place, which almost barred the river, and over and amongst which the river roared and dashed in most glorious style.

The canoe at every transit was taken down very close to these rocks before it caught the back current, and the slightest mismanagement and want of nerve in the ferry-man, would have been instantaneously followed by the inevitable destruction of those crossing. We could thus have crossed ourselves, but any chance of swimming our horses over was entirely out of the question.

The incident was annoying, and ominous at the commencement of our journey, but there was no help for it, so, like Thisbe, we

"Sat and watch'd the waters roll, and more unhappy grew,
At last we echŏ'd with a groan, O dear, what shall we do?"

And, in the words of a Persian philosopher, "contracting the foot of Tranquillity within the mantle of Contentment, and not suffering the collar of Patience to be torn by the hand of Chimera, we smoked the pipe of Spleen on the brink of the river of Disappointment," and abusing rivers in general, but this river in particular, and more than hinting to the ferryman that we considered him to blame for our detention, we had no resource but to retrace our steps over the same ten miles, and ride five or six miles further to the bungalow of one of our companions, whence we were to start next morning, and cross the river some twelve miles lower down.

Next morning we were off again at daybreak, and after a most beautiful forest ride, winding down the precipitous sides of some magnificent grass-clad mountains, with others rising in "solemn amphitheatre" around, and numerous Cingalese villages, and bright enamelled green paddy fields nestling in the hollows and penetrating in terraces one above the other far into the mountain, we reached our friend the River. He or she (for I don't know the gender of Rivers in the East) presented a very different appearance from the day before, and we had the comfort of knowing that if we had exercised a little patience, and waited at the other ferry for a few hours, we might probably have crossed without difficulty, and thus have saved ourselves an unnecessary ride of something under thirty miles. We embarked our horses on a platform between two canoes, and landed them without difficulty.

Our road hitherto had been almost entirely down hill, but directly after crossing the river, we commenced the ascent of the Ramboddy Pass, which continued, without the slightest break or intermission, for some twenty-five miles.

The scenery was equally fine on one side of the river as on the other, but unfortunately the same view seen descending fresh and lively in the cool of the morning, and ascending hungry and tired, scorched and thirsty, towards the afternoon, created very opposite sensations. We had calculated on finding a rest house for the "comfort of man and beast," and had consequently brought neither fluids nor solids with us, but to our disgust we ascertained on arriving at the wished-for spot, that the house of refreshment had been closed some time, and that we had no chance of any refection for the next eighteen miles. I have no doubt that at this stage of the proceedings, a crust of bread and a glass of sherry would have afforded us much more actual pleasure than all the lovely view of the Ramboddy Valley lying at our feet, and stretching for thirty or forty miles, far away in the distance. All mountainous rides, where the road winds up the face, presenting the same view at every turn, must be in some degree monotonous: during the first half-hour the grandeur of the view is continually striking you, and you think you can never have gazed sufficiently on it; the next half-hour your enthusiasm rather cools, and before the expiration of the third (especially, if the roads are bad and your animal unsafe,) you begin to fancy the journey rather tedious, and to wish for a change. This feeling continues increasing till at last you get very tired or very hungry, and all thoughts of the view are forgotten, except as connected with a long, tiresome ride, and your eyes much more probably wander forward to the place of halt than back to the scenery.

The reason why views from a great height become monotonous is simple enough,—there is no change, except that, perhaps, caused by a passing cloud or sunbeam stealing mysteriously over the face of nature; the boundless prospect must be grasped as a whole; you cannot pick out and admire particular beauties; and the mind delighting in variety in everything, the enjoyment of scenery can be kept up for a much longer period, when scenes of comparatively little beauty are constantly recurring, than when one of excessive grandeur is continually presenting itself in unvarying sublimity. It is the same with scenic as with human beauty; variety of expression is far more pleasing than unchanging loveliness of feature.

I don't think I ever remember a more fatiguing ride than this same one up the Ramboddy Pass to Newera Elia; the last ten miles of road winds in quick succession from one side of a ravine to another; all the turns are so exactly similar, and the appearance of the summit of the pass, as seen every now and then, is so deceptive, that the tired traveller begins to fancy he is journeying on the principle of a treadmill, continually moving, but never progressing.

At length, towards dark, with tired backs, tired horses, and tired horsekeepers, we attained the summit; and with renewed spirit rattled down the descent, four or five miles, leading to the plain, or rather the marsh, of Newera Elia.

The far-famed Newera Elia, the sanatorium of Ceylon, 6,200 feet above the level of the sea, was, at the time I was there, the most damp, unpicturesque abode of discomfort I ever remember to have seen. It is a flat, oblong, marshy plain, through which meanders a little stream, surrounded by mountains of about 1,000 or 1,200 feet in height. But that it is green, and the mountains are clad with forests, its shape and size suggest the simile of a vegetable Aden.

CHAPTER XII.

NEWERA ELIA—CLIMATE—MONSOON—FARM STOCK—BADULA.

ALTHOUGH my impressions of Newera Elia in the month of July were anything but agreeable, and my reminiscences even more unsatisfactory, inasmuch as I caught a nasty cold there, I believe that during certain months of the year it is very charming, and that, instead of living literally *in nubibus*, as was the case when I was there, the atmosphere is remarkably clear.

The immediate neighbourhood presents a much more cozy, English appearance than could be expected within ten degrees of the Line, from the settlement and continued residence of two English gentlemen and their families, who, with ample means, have built some excellent houses and farm buildings, thatched and finished in the orthodox style of English farm-houses. They have made considerable clearings, and cultivate potatoes, turnips, carrots, and other European vegetables with tolerable success; they have also established a brewery; but as they have to import malt and hops, empty bottles, &c., from England, and have besides 130 miles of tedious and expensive land carriage, I cannot see how they can ever expect to undersell the London brewers.

The forests on the surrounding mountains are very dense, but present a scrubby, unnatural appearance, neither representing the healthy fibrous vegetation of a temperate, or the luxuriant growth of a tropical climate, but rather a stunted, moss-covered cross between the two, that has crept up, and manages to exist in an uncongenial atmosphere of cold and damp.

A great many elks, and a few cheetah, frequent the woods. The gentlemen I before alluded to, keep a pack of hounds, and regularly hunt the former. It is fatiguing, and not very remunerative sport, inasmuch as the elk invariably takes to water on the first opportunity. Moreover, any hunting that is undertaken in the mountains of Ceylon must be prosecuted on foot; no horse, however small and active, could follow hounds; and I have far too great a respect and affection for that useful hack, Mother Shanks' Mare, ever to attempt to turn her into a hunter.

There is one beauty attending the damp, cold climate of Newera Elia, which is unequalled in the world, viz. the noble growth and gorgeous colours of the different species of rhododendrons. The river I before mentioned is lined with them on both sides, and they present in shape and size the gnarled, knotted appearance of old apple-trees in an English orchard. These trees, at the period of my visit, were thickly covered with large branches of the most brilliant crimson blossoms it is possible to conceive, and which, seen on the dark-green ground of the foliage, or reflected in the crystal stream below, were enchanting, and alone repaid one for the tedious ride, damp beds, and bad dinner of the day before.

The climate of this elevated region is not so useful as a sanatorium in Ceylon as it would be in parts of India. The diseases of the island are chiefly dysentery and other internal ailments, which cold or damp only aggravate; in cases of fever or liver, it would be far more beneficial. There is a small hospital, or rather invalid dépôt, for European soldiers, and I believe it conduces considerably to their health. For persons coming to Newera Elia from Galle or Colombo, the change is very great; in two days you pass from the unmitigated heat of the coast, within eight degrees of the equator, to an intensity of cold that renders fires, blankets, hot brandy and water, not only agreeable, but almost necessary. We, however, had gradually changed our climate by a residence in Kotmalie.

We started early on the 10th, and walked a distance of twelve miles, down hill, to Wilson's bungalow, where we breakfasted. The road was excessively beautiful; and the sensation of swinging comfortably down hill, instead of toiling painfully up, did not render us so hard to please in the way of scenery. We had been told that we should have no rain three miles east of Newera Elia, and such was actually the case. It had rained certainly twenty hours out of every twenty-four, during our stay there and in Kotmalie, and the ground and foliage at the former place were perfectly saturated. The road we were following down towards Badula was for the first three miles almost impassable from mud, when suddenly we came to a line, as distinctly drawn across the road as if the water-carts had ceased their labours at that particular spot. All before us was parched and dried up with an unbroken drought of several months; all behind us saturated and steaming with continued wet of a like duration. You could distinctly see the line kept by the rain-clouds in their rapid course to the north-east, beyond which the sky was blue and unclouded, and held not a single drop of moisture in suspension. The country on either side of the road was mountainous and rugged, and reminded me not a little of Roxburghshire.

We witnessed rather a remarkable meteorological phenomenon on this road, which, though observable in many mountainous countries, is seldom so plainly visible as in Ceylon. The south-west monsoon, getting cool and condensed in traversing the mountains around Newera Elia, was rushing down the ravines and gorges to the parched and glowing plains at our feet with a force that was most remarkable. It blew, not in gusts, as is usual with any very violent force of wind, but with a continuous unbroken stream; so violent was it, that, without exaggeration, those riding felt inclined to dismount, lest horse and all should be blown over the precipice. This wind blows with unceasing force for six months in the year, and renders the country exposed to its fury almost unfit for the residence of human beings, stunting and bowing down all the vegetation as if with a blight.

After breakfasting on bad curry and worse beer, which were only rendered tolerable by the cheroot of digestion, we proceeded on our journey. The road was more cultivated, and water-buffaloes and paddy-fields were frequent. Every paddy-field has its house (like the "lodge in the garden of cucumbers" to be seen in every part of the East to this day), where the proprietors keep watch during the night to frighten off the elephants, pigs, or buffaloes. There is a curious fact connected with the ravages of the elephants on paddy fields, which induces one to imagine that they travel much more than is generally supposed. Although they do not enter the fields when the crop is on the ground, and watch kept, yet they almost invariably make their appearance a day or two after the guard has been removed. This kind of intuitive information is most probably owing to their excessively acute organs of hearing, which is more remarkable with regard to sounds at a distance than to those near at hand.

The great staple of farm stock in the interior of Ceylon consists in herds of water buffalo; they plough the paddy fields, and tread out the corn, and are, in fact, the only animal employed in rice cultivation. They resemble the water buffalo of Egypt and Italy, and like them are endued with the same unpleasant exhalations. They are the most awkward and disgusting of all the bos tribe; they have no hair on their skin whatever, and their hide much resembles, in its colour and appearance, that of the hippopotamus; their horns lying back on their necks, and their noses poked up into the air, give them a most silly appearance. When ploughing belly-deep in the slosh of the paddy fields, or wallowing in the mud and slime, with only their heads and back visible, they are anything but ornamental or picturesque, and when they are lying in the water, which they do whenever they have an opportunity in the middle of the day, with only their nostrils and the crowns of their heads exposed, they present much the appearance of alligators. These ungainly animals are rather savage, and occasionally attack travellers, especially on horseback, and pursue them with great pertinacity.

About ten miles from Wilson's bungalow, we stopped at another bungalow for an hour or so, more for the sake of our horses and horsekeepers than for ourselves. The horsekeepers had run and walked very nearly ninety miles during the last three days, carrying loads and rice of about thirty or forty pounds' weight.

We passed a very primitive bridge over a rapid stream; it was constructed by joining the top branches of two trees on either side the river with withes and bamboos—one strong bamboo for the feet, and two smaller ones some three feet higher, to steady the passenger. It was the most primitive bridge I have ever seen; the natives would seem to have gathered the architectural conception from their prototypes, the monkeys. These latter when they come to a stream, which is too broad for them to spring, hang by each other's tails from a high branch till they have formed a long line, when they commence swinging backwards and forwards, till the monkey at the extremity of the chain manages to catch a bough of the opposite tree, and so form a communication. The females and young ones then pass over this living bridge; sometimes the breadth of the river is not too great for the strong ones to spring across; when two or three crossing over, commence forming a chain on that side also, and thus unite in the centre. I have seen ants form a bridge in precisely the same manner, from one stick to another; I even saw one leave his companions who were clustered at the end of a stick, unable to reach another at a small distance, and making a considerable circuit, ascend the stick they were aiming at, from another direction, and by stretching out his body as far as possible, enabled the pioneer of the main body to reach him, and thus complete the chain of communication, by which the rest immediately crossed: it would be difficult to prove this was not reason!

I had a desperate battle with Punchy regarding some article at a cottage door that he would not pass; force was of no avail, and persuasion was even more useless; he stood alternately on his head and tail, and rubbed my legs against the railing hard by. I wanted to make him pass before the other horses, but I could not effect my purpose, so we had to make a compromise, and let them pass first, when he immediately followed.

Immediately on leaving the second bungalow, you see Badula, or, rather the little valley in which it is lying, close at your feet, and you fancy it is about three or four short miles; but the number and length of the valleys, amongst which the road has to meander in its descent, spins it out to twelve or fourteen very long ones. Every turning you reach you fondly hope must be the last; you see the road perhaps within a stone's throw on the opposite side of the valley, but to reach that you have to traverse one or two miles. I could not help wishing for some aërostatic means of progression, and I longed for the wings of Icarus or his papa. They would have remained firm for that short distance, I imagine.

The Hindoos have a science called Aagiya, which professes to teach them the art of flying: some few try, but fewer still succeed. Combining my experience of yesterday's journey and to-day's, I came to the conclusion that, generally speaking, an unbroken descent is quite as irksome as an ascent of the like duration, and I could not help echoing the sentiment of the camel, who, when asked by the Arab, "Which is the best for you, O camel, to go up hill or down?" answered,

"God's curse light on them both wheresoever they may be found."

The road was excessively tedious, and we did not reach Badula till 8 P. M.; fourteen or fifteen hours on a little pony was too long to be agreeable. The last two hours we progressed entirely in the dark, the only lights visible being those of the stars and the fireflies; these latter are most brilliant and beautiful, and I have never seen them in such numbers, and in such perfection; looking over the declivity of the road, or up in the dark back-grounds of the trees, they formed one lovely mass of scintillating light,—every blade of grass and every leaf was glistering and twinkling, as if the "good folk" were celebrating some joyous festival with a general illumination; and you could almost fancy Queen Mab, in her "state coach, made by the joiner squirrel or old grub," dashing about with her "team of little atomies, and grey-coated waggoner," amongst them. The glow-worm that in England, in the form of a caterpillar, displays its brilliant light during the night, is, as is well known, the disconsolate spouse of some more sprightly lord, that in the graceful and ephemeral form of a moth, is gambolling away in the upper regions; her light is set, like that of Hero, to tempt and direct her absent lover. The firefly, however, is different, as both ladies and gentlemen have the power of emitting light; it is infinitely more beautiful than the glow-worm, inasmuch as it continues flitting and changing its position, enhancing its brilliancy, and rendering the fairy-like illusion more complete.

An imaginative person might construct an allegory of married life from these peculiarities in insects of the same nature. The former, he would compare to the fixed, unchanging affection of the plain, homely wife, constant, and always endeavouring to withdraw her wandering spouse from more seductive attractions; the latter, to the flashing brilliancy of assured beauty, which, careless of all but the admiration of the moment, flits gaily from flower to flower, coveted and caressed, and, like the ignis fatuus, is now dancing before and now behind the object, pursuing, leading him a weary chase, and when secured, proving not unfrequently a disagreeable little insect, with a very sharp sting. Whether is most worthy of admiration, the constant glow-worm or the flirting firefly, I must leave to others of more experience in such matters to determine.

CHAPTER XIII.

BADULA—COOLIES—GIANT OF THE WOODS—MONKEYS—VEGETATION.

BADULA is prettily situated on a plain, at the foot of an amphitheatre of hills; from its position it ought to be healthy, but it is not. When we arrived we found it full of Tamul pilgrims, assembled from the different estates, and even from the coast of India itself, for the annual pilgrimage to Kataragam, all alert to greet some particular sawmy, or god, who was on his way from Kandy on an elephant; the tardiness of his arrival caused some uneasiness to his votaries; however, in the night he came, escorted by a multitude of Gentoos, and proceeded en route to his destination, some sixty miles distant on the east coast. As many as 40,000 pilgrims have been known to assemble at Kataragam; the religious fair—for it deserves no other term, from being frequented by merchants, sharpers, *et id genus*, who resort thither to profit by any stray coin current amongst the pilgrims—occupies a period of some ten or twelve days. The government agent of the district, accompanied by a detachment of rifles, attend to keep the peace,—for large assemblies, even when meeting for the purpose of celebrating the rites of religion, are not always animated by good motives, and at Kataragam serious disturbances have very frequently occurred.

On mustering our "following" next morning, preparatory to commencing the march, I was quite startled at their number. Four of us, carrying each merely one change of raiment, and scarcely any luxuries but liquids, required forty coolies, four horsekeepers, and five servants,—in all fifty men, to attend on four. One saw in a moment how easy it is to account for the millions who are said to have followed Sennacherib and Xerxes, and from the nature of the crowd, one could at once appreciate the ease with which small compact bodies of disciplined men overthrew and annihilated those eastern hordes.

The coolies carry on an average from fifty to sixty pounds, and when tolerably seasoned about the feet, and free from fever, will travel from sixteen to twenty miles a-day for weeks together. They are very willing men, but the most accomplished humbugs imaginable. A cooly will come to you, apparently suffering agonies, if not actually dying, and it requires a very thorough knowledge of the native character, to perceive that it is all affected. Before starting several came to us with complaints, but, as it was out of the question entertaining them at that early period of the proceedings, we dismissed them without any very encouraging notice of their ailments. We administered physic, and that of the most beastly kind procurable, with the most generous profusion; it usually worked a cure by deterring them from attempting the same deception again.

It is not so easy to accomplish a long journey with coolies as might be imagined, as their commissariat, though consisting certainly of rice only, has to be provided for them, either by sending on supplies in advance, or by distributing to each man sufficient for a certain number of days. Their daily allowance is a measure of about two pounds, and on this, to our conception, washy nutriment, they perform considerable marches; the old Spanish proverb, "Tripas llevan a pies," the "feet are carried by the stomach," seems scarcely applicable to them. They all carry curry stuffs of different kinds, and generally manage to pick up some herbs, plantains, cocoanuts, or breadfruit, wherewith to flavour their mess. They boil their rice in the most simple manner, but produce it in a state of perfection that would baffle the most accomplished artiste in

Europe to equal; each grain is distinct and dry, and perfectly soft, in the place of being sloshy and stuck together in lumps as in England. Our coolies had formed messes of threes and fours amongst men of the same caste. They are very particular in respect to eating with any of an inferior caste, and will not touch what has been cooked by a low-caste man.

The chief number of our coolies were Gentoos, who are an offshoot of the Hindoo religion, and most particular in this matter; there were also several Mahrattas from Kandeish, whose caste was very free and easy, and who devoured rotten fish, elephant-gorged pigs, or any other high-seasoned dainties that came to their lot with equal indifference; they were perfectly distinct from the other coolies, both in the cut of their hair and also in not using any ornamental paint.

The Gentoos daub the face with wood ashes, or, if they can procure it, with the ashes of calves' dung boiled in milk. They ordinarily perform this ceremony after meals; it is a propitiatory proceeding in honour of one of their three deities, Brahma, Vishnu, or Seeva: the perpendicular streak is in honour of Seeva, the destroyer; the horizontal one in that of Vishnu, the preserver.

Our coolies, though none of them of very high caste, were distinguished by several minor peculiarities, and observed these distinctions with great care. It is curious to observe the manner in which they eat and drink, never putting the food actually to the lips with the hand, lest the fingers should get contaminated with the saliva. If only a single grain of rice falls from the mouth into the remainder, they have to throw it all away as polluted; consequently they always hold the mouth over the ground when eating, to avoid such a mischance. I think there is a good deal of affectation among the natives in preserving their caste. When any number are together, individuals are afraid to do anything that would disgrace them before others, but when quite alone, I fancy they have no very great scruples of conscience to surmount. Certain castes, such as the Rajpoot, which amongst the Hindus is only secondary to the Brahmin, occasionally insist upon the necessity and the right of being allowed to prepare and consume their victuals in a peculiar manner; since it gives them an opportunity of vaunting their superiority of birth over their companions, and, if they were to do otherwise, they might lose this birthright; but if you remove a Rajpoot from the Bengal to the Madras army, where he will be forced to associate chiefly with low-caste men, he will, after a very short struggle, and in spite of all his threats of self-starvation, fall into the low-caste habits. I fancy if even a Brahmin was sharp set with hunger, and found himself in the position of surreptitiously gratifying his craving with knuckle of ham and a flask of sherry, he would not hesitate very long. —"Publish it not in the streets of Askalon." They themselves have two proverbs to this effect: "To serve his belly, man will play any game;" and "A hungry stomach knows no caste." In drinking at a stream, the coolies illustrate to the letter the description of the three hundred men of Gideon who "lapped, putting their hands to their mouths." Although our followers displayed no want of respect to us, their masters, they nevertheless considered us as low-caste men, all travellers and cripples, *ex officio*, coming under that denomination.

July 12*th*.—Started about daybreak, and marched till about 10 A.M. when we halted for breakfast. Travelling in company with loaded coolies is excessively fatiguing; you cannot progress above two miles and a half an hour, and have to halt continually to give them rest. We passed the track of elephants, the first symptoms of the propinquity of the giant of the woods we had yet seen; we were told they had been trumpeting in considerable numbers during the night, but we had not heard them.

At breakfast we had a slight fracas with the

natives of some neighbouring village, in which the wife of the headman, in the absence of her husband, occupied a very conspicuous part; applying personal observations of the most cutting nature to each of us individually, and to our parents and relations generally: she was an instance of the fact, which I suppose few will be inclined to doubt,—that woman's nature is the same all over the world—angels when amiable, but when enraged, "furens QUID fœmina possit." What, indeed, can they not! The dispute arose about some cocoa-nuts, taken at a low figure by the coolies.

Some of our men had become very foot-sore: it is distressing at first to a greenhorn to watch the exertions of an overloaded coolie, but he very soon gets accustomed to it.

We had a most delicious bathe at breakfast, very refreshing. Here occurred one of those *contre-temps* that attend shooting expeditions. I had brought out with me from England a Prussian needle-gun, that was not only warranted to fire six times a minute, and to cut out a musquitoe's eye at eight hundred yards distance, but was also supposed to enable one to shoot round the corner, and accomplish other feats, which, in the pursuit of large game, would have been highly advantageous. I had experimentalized with it several times, but had always failed; and I confess I felt little confidence in its fitness for actual service. In discharging it at a mark in the river, the whole interior got jammed, and after a useless expenditure of oil and patience, I found it irremediable, and was obliged to send it back by a lame cooly to Badula. It was annoying, as it was my only rifle, and when in good order, is an invaluable weapon.

Encamped about 4 P. M. Our road, during a greater portion of the next day, ran through very close, high jungle: the bush ropes and parasites were of the largest kind I have ever seen; the former could hardly be called ropes, they were rather ten and twelve-inch cables, many of them presenting a twisted appearance, as though some giant of the woods had stranded several together, to make a good cable. They were very long, sometimes stretching from tree to tree, over a distance of several hundred feet. The strain upon them appeared to be very great, and you frequently saw very large trees drawn forcibly together by their power; whilst smaller ones were twisted and distorted, and strangled in their folds, much as you might fancy a huge boa writhing round and crushing a hop-pole.

Humboldt says, that "heat and cold are nature's hands and feet, with which she performs miracles."

If he were to substitute heat and moisture, for heat and cold, I think he would be quite as near the mark. The vegetation of Ceylon is perfectly incredible and continuous. Trees never fall, unless now and then a solitary one, unsupported by parasites, is attacked by wild ants, or struck by lightning. The spot once occupied by nature is never relinquished. An unbroken course of vegetable metempsychosis is continually going on: the original form, indeed, may long ago have ceased, but its vitality is transmitted *ad infinitum*, through lower and successive developments.

The destruction of the giant of the forest, in the vegetable world, through the pernicious influence of the insidious parasite, finds a striking simile in the ruin of man's moral nature in the physical world, through the tyranny of corrupt and enslaving passions. As he attains the strength and importance of maturer years, the useless and destructive habits of the world cling and wreathe around him; unnoticed at first, or perhaps ornamental, neither the animal nor the vegetable makes any exertion to throw them off, till, increasing in strength and number, they wind to the extremity of every limb, and finally cause ruin and desolation, where at first they had excited admiration and envy.

Take another view of it. Man is the strong

tree: woman is the creeper: man's nature is debased or elevated by the nature of the woman he associates with. The creeper naturally seeks the support and shade of the strong tree, and twines and twists, and incorporates itself with it; but how various are its effects upon those trees! Some gentle and lovely, like the myrtle or the honeysuckle, the rose or the verbena, enhance its beauty, harbour the nourishing dews, ward off the scorching heats; whilst others, the ivy and the nightshade, graceful at first, pliant and beautiful, caress only to destroy. Philosophical, very!! A tree destroyed by parasites does not fall: its victorious enemies wind round the strangulated trunk, and binding it together, flower and flourish upon it, as though part of themselves, till in their turn they are attacked and enveloped in the same manner.

July 13th.—The woods were full of monkeys, and as we were sitting at breakfast, thirty or forty of them came galloping along the green avenues, rushing, and springing through the trees with their young ones in their arms, and making a tremendous noise, almost leading the inexperienced imagine that it must be a herd of elephants. Alexander's army once halted on the banks of the Oxus, at the appearance of a multitude of monkeys, which they mistook for the inhabitants of the country, and prepared to give them battle; if they judged of the number and power of the supposed enemy, by the frightful noise they make in the jungle, with their antics and their chattering, it is no wonder the brave Macedonians were alarmed and prepared to defend themselves.

A monkey's life, in a land of perpetual summer, is a very happy one, and I am not sure that those miserable objects, caged and confined at the Zoological Gardens, do not feel their loss of liberty as much, if not more, than the larger animals. There are many kinds of monkeys in Ceylon; some are of a considerable size; and Bishop Heber even speaks of one that attacked a friend of his, and broke his gun-barrel. (One cannot doubt, a Bishop!) In days long past, the island is said to have been conquered by an Emperor of Sumatra, with an army of monkeys.

The vegetation was excessively luxuriant, especially as regarded ferns and palms, many of the former attaining a size that would scarcely be credited in England. I measured several tree ferns, that at a distance of twelve or fourteen feet from the ground, were three and four feet in circumference, and at least thirty feet high; they do not at all resemble the graceful tree ferns of the South American mountains, but rather the arborescent ferns that are supposed to have abounded so largely in the carboniferous era of the secondary period. The grasses also of the low country of Ceylon attain an enormous size, not unfrequently being twenty feet in height.

CHAPTER XIV.

RUINS—ANTS—JACK-FRUIT—TICKS—PARK OF CEYLON—ELEPHANT SHOOTING—ENCAMPMENT.

WE passed several high tombs, of a conical rather than a pyramidal shape, and apparently of great antiquity, composed of stones placed carelessly together. Ceylon abounds in ruins of this nature, from pyramids nearly equal to those of Sakkara, down to the little cairns or heaps of stones, which the piety or superstition of the natives has raised upon the sites of death or burial. Some of the ruins are on the largest scale, and have moreover the recommendation of comparative novelty, as having been only recently brought under the notice of civilized man. Those of the city of Anarajahpoorah are on a scale of magnificence, that in a country like Ceylon, which can at present boast of so little energy and so scanty a population, is very surprising. The only reasons why these remains of ancient grandeur are not so interesting as those of Egypt or Assyria, is that they are totally unconnected with any historical associations. In that respect they resemble those of Yucatan, or the Tumuli and buried cities of North America, without, however, sharing the peculiar attraction of those cities, viz. mystery.

The history of these recently-discovered cities in Ceylon, from the date of their foundation to that of their desertion, about A. D. 600, has been translated from the Palee, by Turner; but they were built, inhabited, and destroyed by such an uninteresting race, that it is quite impossible to work up the smallest degree of enthusiasm about them.

However, wonderful as may be the remains of human industry, they are almost equalled by the untiring energy and gigantic structures of the ants. The height and dimensions of their sugar-loaf, volcano-looking abodes, are really surprising. I have sat, whilst on horseback, alongside of one, which was higher by some feet than my head, and they frequently raise them to the height of twelve or fourteen feet, in that respect exceeding the white ant of the mainland of India. These dwellings are 1,500 times higher than the creatures themselves—at this rate our buildings ought to be thirty-five or forty times higher than the Monument in London, and twelve times higher than the Pyramids of Egypt, to attain a like proportionate height.

The white ants are truly the most extraordinary of all the formican tribe; they do not resemble other ants in their appearance or nature, but are more like small white slugs on legs, rather slow in their movements, and very soft, and are said to be delicious eating. A Mr. Smeathman, who studied their habits and flavour on the coast of Guinea, compares them to sugared cream, and the paste of white almonds! Some castes of Cingalese certainly eat them voraciously, so I suppose there must be a peculiar kind of gusto about them.

The routine of their existence and the termination of it, are strongly contrasted; they toil and moil below, in raising enormous fabrics and undermining the mighty trees of the forest, when all of a sudden they are endowed with wings, and immediately ascend off the ground in a cloud, attempting to soar to the upper sky; but whether it is that their gossamer propellers are not powerful enough to support their fat white carcasses, or that their instincts are not sufficiently matured to enable them to adapt themselves to their new mode of life, I cannot say; certain it is that their flight is very short, and anything but enjoyable; all the birds of the air attack them, and the slightest shower of rain, or the mildest rays of the sun, are equally fatal. Their flight scarcely ever lasts more than an hour, when they fall, *en masse*, helpless and pulpy, to be the prey of every "critter," flying or creeping, that has a taste for sugared cream and almond paste!

Generally speaking, the ants are republicans, and in that respect are opposed in their constitution to the bees. "The ants' republic, and the realm of bees" is a general distinction marked by Pope, but it is not universally true, and the termites, or white ants, form the exception. Amongst them the office of universal mother and wetnurse is undertaken by some enterprising young ant, with a strong development of the organ of philoprogenitiveness; when selected for her great feat in the maternal line, she is of ordinary size, and perhaps of a graceful appearance, but before the termination of the business, she attains the size of a man's thumb, and is 1,000 times larger than her lord the king; she is placed in a cell, which is enlarged, day by day, as she increases in bulk, and there she produces as many as *thirty-one millions* of eggs. The Annales Fuldensis relate a story of a certain Margaretta, Countess of Wensberg, who brought forth 365 children at once; but that is a number scarcely worth noticing in the present case. The appearance she presents to her loyal subjects, when in this unnatural state of distension, is the most disgusting thing I know in nature: the small legs and head of an ordinary ant are just visible on the huge, white, festering-looking mass which is covered all over with incisions like the slashings of a diminutive white satin sleeve in olden days, whence the eggs exude; whether the queen ever recovers her health, or resumes her former size, I cannot take upon myself to say, but I should think it doubtful. One of the most ancient writers on India, Ctesias, describes the ants as being as large as foxes; he must have formed his opinion either from the size of their mounds, or from a specimen of the queen herself, when in an interesting condition. If he was told that the latter was one of a family of thirty-one millions produced at a birth, and which would indeed be perfectly correct, instead of the mother of that number, he might surely picture to himself an animal as large as a fox or even as an elephant!

In tropical climates the ants not only serve the office of scavengers, which they perform with much more neatness and cleanliness than the beetles do in our colder regions, but they are capital barometers. When you see a community of them hurrying about at speed in all directions, laden with their cocoons and stores, you may be sure rain is near at hand. They appear an equally hard-working, provident race, as the English ant, storing with as much care and activity their provision against the *wet* as ours do against the *frosty* season.

If the sole distinction between instinct and

reason does actually lie in the connexion of "remembrance and reflection," and the narrow division that separates "sense from thought," which, as the most philosophical of English poets remarks,—

> "long to join,
> But never pass the insuperable line,"

it would really appear as if the natural gifts of the ant actually embraced these four senses: experience derived from the remembrance of past seasons; reflection as to how to provide for those to come; the sense of their insecurity visible in the thought they take to render their abodes strong and unapproachable,—all seem to give them a high mental standard: and although it is undeniable that the bees have done more for science, by solving the famous mathematical problem of maxima and minima, and demonstrating, in the construction of their cells, the particular angle at which three planes must meet, so as to combine the greatest possible strength with the least possible loss of space, yet the ants appear bolder, and more solid in their architecture. As architects, they bear much the same resemblance to the bees as the builders of the pyramids do to those of Milan cathedral, or the Taj-Mahal.

There is a remarkable similarity, according to naturalists, in the internal economy of the "ant republic," and the great human republic of our age. They are both the most energetic and untiring of their species, and apparently are both rather unscrupulous in the means they employ for their aggrandisement: they are both slave-holders, and I have no doubt, if any Philo-Formican Abolitionist Society were to arise amongst the insects, they would receive much the same respect and consideration as the like community does amongst the human ants of America. There is little doubt that half the great works of the ant are the result of forced labour: it has been ascertained by Mr. Hanhault, Mr. Hubert, junior, and others, that their wars, which are fierce, scientific, and continuous, are carried on not for food, as was imagined, but merely for the purpose of seizing the cocoons and young ants from their neighbours, and taking them home, to rear them up as public bondsmen, to build and repair the public property, whilst they enjoy the old feudal privilege of idling or fighting. It does not yet appear whether they have arrived at the enlightened stage of the human ant in purchasing and bartering their slaves, or whether they may not henceforth adopt some plan of getting them by arbitration.

The natives supplied us with some most delicious plantains, of that small, sweet nature peculiar to the East; they also brought in some gigantic jack-fruit. This last is the largest edible fruit in the world, often attaining a weight of fifty and sixty pounds. I could not appreciate its flavour, though it is much relished by many persons. It is excessively fattening for cattle, and the seeds contained in the fruit, when smashed together and boiled, bear a striking resemblance to potatoes. The fruit is not produced at the extremity of the branches, as is the case with most fruit-bearing trees, or even on the branches at all, but is attached to the trunk itself by a short rope-like stalk, excessively strong and fibrous. The providence of nature is very remarkable in the production of this Brobdignagian fruit: as the tree advances in age, the fruit is year by year produced lower on the trunk, till, from being almost at the summit of the young trees, it is found but a very few feet above the ground in the old ones. By that means, the tree itself is not endangered by the top weight of such enormous fruit, and the fruit itself saved from the utter "*smash*" which must attend its fall from any great height.

We put up in a kind of bungalow, made of plantain, cocoa-nut leaves, and bamboos. It was rather a pretty spot, and the Æolian-like sound of the leaves of the royal cocoa-nut trees gently clashing in the evening breeze round our bungalow, was very singular, and most cool and refreshing. The headman of the district paid us a visit, and, although a Buddhist, drank off a remarkably stiff horn of brandy with the greatest complacency, from that time indulging in a stream of volubility that seemed to astonish his "tail."

This was the first place where we became acquainted with that curse of Ceylon, hardly secondary to the leeches, viz. ticks. They are hard minute insects, varying in size from a pin's head to about five times that size. They resemble little crabs, and, like them, are armed with the most cruel forceps, which they use with astonishing power. They appear to live in families, and to inhabit particular cavities and holes. You may be in a camp two or three days without one, when by accident, perhaps, you disturb a family party, and in the next second are covered with them. The first intimation you have of their presence is a sharp itch, and if you do not on the instant take off the insect, the itch is succeeded by a twinge, which increases in intensity, till if, as is usually the case, the tick has managed to fix upon some tender part, such as the quick under the nail, or between the toes, it becomes almost unbearable. I verily believe that if Lord Chesterfield, Beau Brummel, or any other stickler for etiquette past or present, were to be attacked on the sole of the foot, or between the toes, by a tick, he would be compelled to haul off shoe and stocking, though in full costume, and in the presence of royalty itself. The ticks punish the horses most severely and cruelly, and keep them awake for whole nights.

Our coolies were sleeping all around our bungalow, and during the night they awoke us, to say that some Cingalese were in the room, probably thieving. It was not at all likely, inasmuch as there were four of us sleeping in the same room; and any intruder would have had a poor chance of getting out with a sound skin. However, the Cingalese are very expert thieves, and about Colombo proceed to their work *in puris naturalibus,* well oiled, and without even a rag which can afford an opportunity of catching hold of them.

We witnessed, to-day, a very primitive method adopted by the Cingalese in computing distances. When asked how far it is to such and such a place? they say, two or three *calls,* meaning thereby, two or three times the distance at which one man can hear another call; of course this would vary considerably with the direction of the wind, and strength of the individual's lungs, but on an average, I fancy a call is heard about half a mile off. The old saying of the Campbells, "'tis a far cry to Lochow," seems almost to imply that they formerly measured distances in the same manner.

During the night the roar of elephants had

been heard in all directions, but the experienced leader of our party declined remaining to hunt, as the trackers of the district were indifferent and exorbitant in their charges, and the jungle exceedingly bad and impracticable, so we started early the next day through the Bintenne country for the Park, our path lying through some magnificent forests, stocked with legions of monkeys. The guide insisted on the probable appearance of a "rogue" elephant, who, he said, infested the road and did a great deal of harm; he feigned the utmost alarm, and kept looking for him at every turn. At our first halt, under a *Ficus indicus*, or banyan-tree, the coolies began scraping the bark to make the tree bleed, and when sufficient juice had oozed to the surface, they applied it to the cracks on their feet. Many were suffering terribly from this cause; the deep scorching sand of the paths and watercourses we had to follow, alternating with hard roads of the smallest sharpest quartz, having cut their feet most cruelly, and indeed the horses suffered also.

We passed a regular Druidical circle of stones, about three feet high. It would appear from these remains, so frequently found in India and Ceylon, that the Druidical form of worship, which is supposed to have been that of the Phœnicians, and to be emblematical of the sun, and traces of which have been discovered in every part of the known world, existed likewise to a considerable extent in the far east.

About eight o'clock, we entered the far-famed "Park," a meet as well known to sportsmen of Ceylon as Billesdon Coplow is to those of the midland counties. It is a magnificent country, resembling Richmond-park in the rise and fall of the land, and in the quantity and appearance of the scattered forest. You might take 500 acres out of any spot, and place it in a midland county of England, with a gentleman's seat upon it, and the only remark it would elicit, would be, what a very beautiful park!

The foliage of the trees is not tropical when seen at a short distance, rather resembling that of oaks and chestnuts; but the grass is certainly un-English in appearance, as in ravines and damp localities, it grows to the height of fifteen or twenty feet. The Park covers about thirty square miles of country; the soil is scanty, and consequently the pasture is only good immediately after the rains; it was formerly as well stocked with elephants at certain seasons of the year, as Richmond-park is with deer; indeed, Major Rogers shot the greater proportion of his 1,300 or 1,500 in that district. It is especially fitted for elephant shooting, as you have plenty of cover under which to approach, and a sufficient number of trees to afford protection, without the dangerous jungle to entrap you. The sport is there enjoyed in perfection; you go to work with a certain knowledge of what you will have to perform, having a good look at the elephants, how many there are, and the best way of getting near them; whereas, in the jungle, you do not probably see them till they are within ten or twelve yards of you, and the moment you have fired, they are lost to sight. The district, however, is by no means so plentifully supplied with elephants now as formerly; they have been so harassed and thinned in number, that except just at the time when the young grass is springing up, very few resort there. For the abundance of all other game, deer, wild buffalo, and hog, the Park is still unrivalled; the ground seems made for stalking; slight undulations and hollows, alternating with patches of jungle, assist the sportsman in every way; and I have no doubt a good shot, well acquainted with the country, might make a larger bag there of deer and hog than in any other part of the world.

However, as in England, every kind of game, and any quantity of it, is immediately relinquished for the chance of a woodcock; so, in Ceylon, shooting parties go out solely for the purpose of shooting elephants, and neglect all smaller game, frequently to their own subsequent sorrow and mortification, when, instead of returning with a good game list of buck and buffalo, they have only one *tail* to show as the result of a week's sport; and very probably not even that!

We camped about 3 P.M. in a small patch of jungle, on the bank of a rapid stream, and directly we had halted, each one of the party started off in a different direction with his attendant tracker, to try and pick up a stray buck or so. I worked uncommonly hard, and hurried after a long lanky slip of a boy over an amount of ground, and at a speed that was excessively warming, and otherwise unremunerative. My friend, unencumbered with any clothes whatever, glided along up and down hill, through thicket and high grass, in the most aggravating manner. I could not explain to him my sentiments on the subject of a more moderate progression, as the moment I spoke he stopped short, and when I gave the signal to proceed, went on again faster than ever. We saw several herds of deer, and sounders of hog, but could not manage to get a shot; the park was burning all around, and the animals were restless, and on the move. On my return, I fell in with two of my companions, and found they had been equally unsuccessful, and equally hurried and heated. We were in great want of some fluid to imbibe, and not being able to gratify our craving in any other manner, we attacked a cocoa-nut-tree, and commenced firing at the nuts; we broke several, and got milky shower baths, but were also fortunate in bringing down two or three unbroken. The juice of the young cocoa nut is most delicious and refreshing to a thirsty soul, and what is of great importance in that treacherous climate, is perfectly innocuous.

The approach to our camp was extremely picturesque; our tents hanging from the trees, the numerous cooking fires of the coolies casting a red glare upon the surrounding forest, the horses picketed close by, with their swarthy attendants squatted round, discussing their day's work, or evening meal, combined to form a striking picture.

After a few weeks' camping out in the East, the novelty and beauty of the different groupings, brilliant colouring, and *peculiar character* of Indian scenery, fail to attract any particular attention, but to a *griff* fresh from England, they cannot but at first appear highly interesting and picturesque.

This was our first regular night under canvass, and when we were turning into comfortable beds, with pillows and musquito curtains, in a good-sized tent, after a good, almost a luxurious dinner, of curry and rice, beer and sherry, I and one of my companions could not help comparing notes, and remembering the last time we had camped out together in the prairies of North America, where, without fire or tent, with a thermometer below zero, no beer, no sherry, in fact no nothing, we had thought ourselves fortunate in having a piece of tough wolf, or tougher bull to masticate, and in finding a spot at all sheltered from the piercing wind and driving snow, where we might roll ourselves up in our buffalo robes, with some prospect of not finding ourselves dead men in the morning!

There is certainly far more luxury in the East, but you miss the independence, and the light, exhilarating sensation, arising from the sense of perfect health; on the prairies, you are braced up above your average standard of energy and spirits, in the East you sink just as much below it.

Coolies are curious creatures; every day during the march they appeared so lame and exhausted, that we almost expected to be obliged to send some of them home, but no sooner had they swallowed their rice in the evening, than they began to laugh and sing; and whenever any soft ground gave them the opportunity, they would play at a most riotous, fatiguing game, something like our prisoner's base, frequently till past midnight.

CHAPTER XV.

BURNING PARK—VEDDAHS—CONDAVETTAM—ELEPHANTS.

July 14*th*.—In consequence of the wildness of the game, from the burning of the park, which the natives set on fire every year to furnish new grass, we were obliged to move off; and procuring a couple of guides from the head man for the Batticaloe district, we broke up camp, and started at 8 A.M. for the next halting place. About 10 we reached the part that was on fire, and marched on during the rest of the day with burning forests on all sides of us, sometimes too close to be perfectly agreeable, and more than once we had to wait on ground already burned, till the fire before us had consumed the high grass through which it had to pass. There is no danger, as is the case on the prairies of North America, for the neighbourhood of the trees prevents the fire spreading with any very great rapidity; but still sometimes, in the ravines, and amongst the high jungle and Cufa grass, twelve or twenty feet high, it crackled and roared in grand style. Our path lay through some very wild intricate gorges, with craggy overhanging rocks on either side, and the fire darting and shooting amongst the crevices, had a very singular and beautiful effect.

The low country of Ceylon was at this time very unhealthy, in consequence of the excessive drought, and nearly all the natives we met were suffering more or less from fever; they are far more subject to this complaint than Europeans, which is generally the case with fever and ague all over the world.

During the night, there arose a violent storm of wind, and it required a certain amount of nerve to sleep serene, with the knowledge that many probably of the gigantic trees around, were mined and hollowed by white ants, and that any extra gust might bring them down upon us. We were off into the Park before daybreak, for the purpose of supplying the pot. I discarded the active, long-limbed youth of the day before, and placed myself under the guidance of a more staid, and less impulsive tracker. We saw many herds of deer and hog, and also some wild buffalo; but all the game was so wild, in consequence of the close proximity of the fire, that any chance of a successful stalk was out of the question. I was much amused with watching the manœuvres of some large monkeys, who apparently were equally gratified with their inspection of me.

The country I shot over was much the same as that of the day before, and I frequently could not help fancying I was sneaking and poaching in some gentleman's park or pheasant covers in England.

On returning to camp about midday, I found that two of the party had been successful, and that a buck and doe were the fruits of their sporting labour. According to Scripture, "The slothful man roasteth not that which he took in hunting." We, I believe, laid ourselves under the same imputation, but not for the same reason; we did not eat our game, for the very good reason that we could never have masticated or chewed it had we had it cooked ever so nicely. In the tropics, neither game nor domestic animals afford at all the same quality of food as in temperate climes; in fact, they are so dry and stringy, as to be almost useless for culinary purposes.

We were out again directly after breakfast, and hunted till dark without success. Just as I returned to camp I tumbled on a very large porker, he was the largest I had seen, and was actively engaged in the pursuit of roots when I first saw him; I crept as near to him as I could, but the evening had so far closed in, and the light was so bad, that though I fired with the deliberate intention of committing murder, my shot only tumbled him over, and I had the mortification of seeing him recover his understandings, and scuttle off into the jungle before I could seize the opportunity of administering the *coup de grace*.

Being anxious to reach elephant ground, we struck camp again on the 16th, and marched for Nicavelly, twelve miles distant. The road lay chiefly through forest; some of the trees were magnificent, especially the cotton-tree, which, with a perfectly erect stem of sixteen or eighteen feet in circumference, attains a height of between forty and fifty feet without throwing out a branch, and with its graceful purple flowers, presents a very beautiful object.

About midday we halted for a delicious bathe. In the evening I was startled by what I thought was the cry of a deer close to camp, though the animal that emitted the sound was evidently moving about so rapidly, that I knew at once that it could not be one. On inquiry it proved to be a flying fox, whose cry is a sharp, though not unpleasing one, much resembling that of a deer.

17*th.*—Lifted camp very early; our startings usually took place by moonlight, or in the very early dawn; they were occasionally excessively picturesque, and conducted with as much regard as possible to our individual comfort, the "Sahibs" not being roused till tea and coffee were ready, and whilst they were consuming the invigorating beverage, the tents and beds were taken down, guns loaded, horses saddled, and the march commenced.

The headman of the district was our guide, a handsome man, with more character and decision about his features than belongs to most of his race, and moreover he wore no comb. The double-barrelled rifle he carried was the gift of some sportsman whom he had attended and tracked for, and his reputation for great presence of mind, when at close quarters with elephants, stood very high. He was attended by a low caste Cingalese, one of the wilder tribes, who live entirely in the jungle. This man was darker than the other natives, and very uncouth in his manner. The tribe to which he belonged still hunt, and bring down the elephant and other wild animals, with the bow and arrow. They shoot elephants either behind the shoulder, or, like Paris, they strike the otherwise invulnerable monster in the heel; of course, in neither case is death instantaneous, but when the animal is once stricken, they will follow the trail for days, until he falls.

There is another and even a wilder race, of whom we met two one day, called Veddahs, and most extraordinary stories are circulated respecting them, such as their living in trees, having tails, and being, in fact, half monkey in appearance, and more than half monkey in habits; it is humanity in the transition state, establishing at once Lord Monboddo's theory of elongated spines, or the "successive emanation" philosophy of more recent *savants*. Some have supposed them to be descendants of that army of monkeys, with red faces and black beards, who, commanded by Hunooman, the Indian Pan, (who, by the bye, broke his cheek-bone in a fall from the sun's orbit,) came over from India, and conquered Ravan, king of the giants, and sovereign of Ceylon. "The ape is a merry and bold beast," says Bacon. Their descendants, the Veddahs, appear entirely to have lost these social qualities. All these reports regarding the Veddahs are imaginary; they are much the same as other species of the human race, with the exception of being small, which probably arises from the unhealthiness of the districts they have for generations inhabited, and from poverty and scarcity of nourishment. Living in a country which is frequently overrun by elephants, they are doubtless obliged occasionally to take refuge in the trees, but that these are not their ordinary habitations, may be proved from the fact of their possessing huts and temporary villages, and cultivating their plantains, much as the other races of Ceylon. They speak a language but very slightly understood by the Cingalese themselves, they never marry out of the tribe, and avoid as much as possible all intercourse with the natives. They are probably the remnant of an Aboriginal race that formerly inhabited Ceylon, and their small stature may be, as I before remarked, the effects of hard living and unhealthy climate. They appear to bear some affinity to the Dyaks of Borneo, in their manners and customs, and seem to belong to that diminutive family of the human race, of whom the diggers of New Mexico, the Bushmen of Africa, and some tribes in India, are individuals. It is not likely that any one will take the trouble of studying the lingo of the Veddahs, and they will probably ere long die off, and leave the forest in undisturbed possession to their companions, the bears and elephants.

Long march of twenty miles to a place called Condivettam. The jungle for the greater part of the way was so dense and intricate, and the elephant tracks so numerous and confusing, that without a guide well acquainted with the country, any hope of penetrating it would have been useless. During the day we came upon a village, and passed through acres of plantain and breadfruit-trees, entirely destroyed by a herd of elephants, only a night or two before. Like the boys and the frogs, what is fun to the strong animal, is death to the weak.

The natives, indolent and helpless, depend entirely upon the generosity of their Mother Earth to produce year after year the fruits upon which they expect to exist; but they take no means to ensure a supply, or to protect what Nature in her abundance produces.

The banana or plantain of the tropics, both in the East and West Indies, is the most munificent and prodigal of all Dame Nature's gifts. It is unknown in a totally uncultivated state; but the profusion with which it repays the slightest attention is astonishing. It is estimated, that on the same space of ground, the banana produces something like a hundred and thirty times the bulk of wheat, and about forty-five times that of potatoes. I mean, of course, of wheat and potatoes grown in climates suited to them. A fine bunch of bananas with thirty or forty fruit, all of the same rich golden hue, presents a very magnificent appearance; when left to nature, the lowest fruit on the branch ripens first, and becomes yellow, whilst the others are still green; but the Cingalese and the natives of India have a method of burying the bunch for a short time, when they require a perfect one for a feast or a wedding, which causes all the fruit to assume the same hue at the same time.

The larger description of banana, though the finest specimen of tropical fruit, is not nearly so palatable as a small fruited banana, called scientifically "Musa sapientium," from having been from time immemorial the favourite food of the philosophers and Brahmins of India. It is truly a most delicious fruit, and, eaten with milk and sugar, bears a considerable resemblance to strawberries and cream.

We had now got regularly into the elephant country; their spoor, and the destructive effects of their gambols or rage, were visible in every direction. They had been roaring continually in the neighbourhood, and our guide fully expected to see them every instant. A little trepidation was perceptible accordingly amongst some of the most timid of the coolies: they had not exactly reached the state when the "sound of a shaken leaf should chase them," but the crashing of every flock of monkeys, before unheeded, now caused a halt, and preparations for a retreat, at the expense of loads and everything else. At length the trackers, who had gone on in front, returned at a trot, saying they saw elephants. We hurried back with them to the bed of a very broad river perfectly dry, and at the distance of a mile or so they pointed out two animals moving about, but whether they were elephants or buffaloes we could not determine. It was too late to commence the campaign that night, as we should have been obliged to make a considerable circuit through the jungle to get the wind of them.

The route to our camping ground lay down the river, the soft deep sand of which was thickly covered with elephant foot-marks. We were excessively thirsty, and gladly availed ourselves of the wells which these sagacious brutes had scooped out in the sand, to collect the water that was dribbling through the arenaceous bed of the stream. They scratch holes three or four feet deep with their feet, and then wait patiently till the water accumulates, taking especial care when drawing out the water with their trunks to keep at the greatest possible distance, so as not to allow their weight to shelve in their temporary means of supply.

The elephant, like many heavy men, is painfully alive to his great weight, and to the danger he incurs from trusting it on anything at all fragile; he generally sounds the strength of anything doubtful with one foot, and if not perfectly satisfied with the trial, no amount of persuasion or force will induce him to trust himself upon it.

Winding up a long hot march of twenty miles,

with three miles of deep burning sand, was punishing work for the coolies, and I fully expected some would have broken down. About a mile down the bed of the river, we passed the carcass of an elephant, a young one, that had been killed by the Moormen of Condivettam, for the sake of its tusks, which it possessed of a larger size than usual. The stench was something quite fearful, and even galloping past as fast as I could, it very nearly stifled me. I can quite understand the legend of the dead snake I have before alluded to, causing a pestilence amongst the Roman troops in Africa.

This elephant was one of two the Moormen had captured for the Rajah of Travancore, who sends over some Arabs every year to purchase them. The Ceylon elephants, although a few inches lower in the shoulder, are stronger, more active, and more intelligent than those of the mainland; they have also more courage when exposed to fire, and were always ridden by the great magnates of India. It is said that the Indian elephants salaam to their brethren of Ceylon, in deference to their superior merits.

The manner of catching them is simple enough, and, with the stealthy, cat-like peculiarities of the Moormen of Ceylon, is attended with little danger. When a herd has been discovered, in which there are young ones, they watch them till mid-day, when they are either drowsy or asleep, and then creeping up behind with ropes, fasten their hind legs together; they then set up loud yells and fire guns, to frighten away the old ones. The course of education afterwards pursued is very simple, but speedy and effective: they are left tied, with no water or food, for three or four days, when these requisites are administered as sparingly as possible: in a week, they become so tractable as to kneel down and rise up at the word of command.

We camped in the forest at the edge of the river of sand, about a mile from the Moormen's village, and in the evening I went to see the young prisoner. He had only been captured three days, and his rage had by no means diminished. Secured between two trees, he attempted to charge everything that approached, and the concentrated fury visible in his little eyes, which, ludicrously small in proportion to his size, seemed starting out of his head, was very remarkable. The Moormen expected to get 7*l.* or 8*l.* for him from the afore-mentioned Rajah of Travancore.

CHAPTER XVI.

MOSQUITOS—DEVIL-BIRD—OUR FIRST ELEPHANT—FIRST SENSATIONS ON ENCOUNTERING AN ELEPHANT — A JUNGLE CUISINE — MORE ELEPHANTS—QUESTIONABLE BEDFELLOW.

CEYLON is certainly a land of contradictions. We had frequently camped in swamps of most ominous appearance, and had closed our mosquito nets with suspicious care, when, to our surprise, not an enemy appeared; while here, on the banks of a dry stream, with not a drop of water to generate the race, we were attacked in the most cruel manner. Venus Anadyomene, rising from the sea, was the original type of the mosquito: like her, the insect springs ephemeral and beautiful from the water, leaving its shell behind; and, once fairly launched into this upper world, never ceases from stinging and tormenting miserable humanity, when an occasion offers. It is not, perhaps, generally known that, as with us, it is the female only that stings; and though one occasionally hears, one does not certainly often credit, the accounts of the "stings of love," originating with the male portion of creation. Woman is generally the mosquito; man the inflammatory victim, who tries, though generally in vain, with the mosquito net of mysogynism, or the smudges and tobacco-smoke of bachelor habits, to ward off their invidious attacks: however, it is the same with the mosquitos as with the fair sex; if the defence is not *quite* perfect and impervious it is utterly useless: the presence of even one buzzing and triumphant, often does more to banish rest and quiet than the presence of a hundred.

We slept very little that night; and my companion, driven to desperation, at last rushed out into the centre of the stream, and there rolling himself in his blanket, sought in the more open space a refuge from the merciless attacks of our persecutors.

During the evening, our coolies, and especially the Cingalese servants, had exhibited great signs of alarm at the continued call of the devil-bird: it is a most unearthly, discordant sound, supposed to portend misfortune to those who hear it, and as our campaign was expected to commence the following day, they were impressed with the conviction that one, if not more, of the "sahibs" would probably fall a victim to the rage of some infuriated "rogue."

We had sent out trackers over night, and early in the morning were all prepared, with guns loaded and horses saddled, ready to start in any direction that might be deemed advisable. About seven, our men came in exhausted with haste, and reported a herd of elephants about three miles off. We started at once, and rode down the bed of the stream for a mile or so, when, leaving it, we struck through the jungle, to a large ruined tank, of about four miles long and two broad. It was covered with the beautiful red lotus, and all around it, and at the edge of the jungle, were herds of wild hog and flocks of peacocks feeding. The morning was most lovely, and the scene one of exceeding beauty, so calm and tropical in its deep repose; the view bounded by the dark impervious forest in the foreground, the purple, hazy outline of the mountains around Badula seen in the extreme distance, the unclouded sky, with not a breath to disturb the perfect tranquillity that overspread all nature, combined to form a scene, which I think I shall remember much longer than the sporting adventures with which it was connected.

We were afraid to fire at the smaller game, lest we should alarm the nobler quadrupeds: when about half-way up the tank, we descried an old "rogue" bathing himself in the muddy water; he was some distance off, and as our trackers had brought us out to see a herd and not a single elephant, and, moreover, insisted upon the truth of their report, we left the old gentleman to his ablutions, and, dismounting, examined our caps and nipple powder; and then, the word being given, we advanced in single file, preceded by the trackers, in the supposed direction of the animals.

The trackers displayed the most obvious signs of uneasiness; and Duff, who was an experienced hunter, more than once whispered his conviction that there was no herd whatever, but that we were being inveigled into attacking a "rogue." After about a quarter of an hour's progression in solemn silence through the densest of jungles, the trackers stopped and gave us to understand that an elephant was close to us. The jungle was so thick and entangled, we could not see five yards ahead of us, and could only move with difficulty: we therefore had to wait, and see if time would discover our friend. Our patience was not long tried—he had heard our approach, and by unmistakeable sounds well known to elephant hunters, gave token of uneasiness and alarm. After crashing about in the jungle with the noise and snort of a railway engine, he expressed his animosity in a shrill trumpet,* and bore right down towards us. As

* The trumpet of an elephant is a most startling portentous sound, and only emitted when he is highly enraged.

we could see nothing, we prepared to give him a volley; however, he, evidently, was not aware either of our confined position or of his own enormous power, for when within ten yards, and still invisible, though we could see the jungle bending, he turned sharp off, in another direction. We followed as fast as we could; and, guided by the trackers, in about ten minutes again approached his neighbourhood: we had made a kind of circuit, and in consequence of his having scented us in one direction, and heard us in another, he had got confused, and did not, as is usual when an elephant wishes to escape, make right off. The former scene was reenacted several times, and he treated us thus cavalierly for two or three hours, till at last, judging by his reckless charges, and continued trumpetings and snortings, he got into a most uneasy and unenviable state of mind, and after approaching us very closely, he all at once retreated as noiselessly as a cat. This noiseless progress of elephants is one of the most striking things connected with the sport; when disturbed, a herd will crash away with a frightful din, but when they have got ten or twenty yards, all sound ceases, and the inexperienced hand advances with the utmost caution, thinking they have halted, when in reality they are half-a-mile off. The softness of their feet, and their enormous size, which enables them to press down twigs and branches without breaking them, and the wonderful facility with which they push aside the opposing branches with their trunks, must account for this.

Our first attempt was thus unsuccessful, but it was unavoidable, and we were lucky to have escaped as well as we did. The jungle was far too thick, and it is an acknowledged axiom amongst elephant hunters never to enter a very bad jungle to attack a single elephant: the bush-ropes and tangled underwood that offer no opposition whatever to his colossal tread, effectually stop and hamper a "human," either in his retreat or attack.

Maréchal Saxe said no man ever snuffed a candle with his fingers without experiencing the sensation of fear; and I don't think many get over their first interview with an enraged elephant, without realizing the same sensation in a greater or less degree. "Fear," with whatever amount of ludicrous pertinacity men are wont to repudiate its existence, is quite a natural feeling, and has existed, and will exist, in all ages of the world. The Athenians and others deified it, as they did all the passions that were implanted by Nature, and I think that the propinquity of an awkward customer, like the one I have mentioned, might well give a green hand a sufficient excuse for sacrificing to that deity. In nine cases out of ten, fear arises from the want of habit and confidence; and with the frequent recurrence of the original cause of alarm, the sense of danger soon diminishes, till it almost becomes one of indifference. The sailor, for instance, will go aloft with perfect composure in a gale of wind, while the soldier, who is bent upon seeking the "bubble reputation," at any hazard, on shore, would most decidedly decline making the experiment. It is the same in the delicate business of "popping the question;" a man's first proposals are made with excessive timidity, he is bolder the second time, and having escaped so far, and convinced himself of how little real danger attends the experiment, he will afterwards, with perfect nonchalance, go through a scene, that brings a much braver man's heart in his mouth merely to think of. It is the same with elephant shooting: the first time it is certainly nervous work, the second less so, till with a little practice a man with ordinary nerves approaches an elephant with very little more dread or excitement than he does a doe or a pig.

We returned to camp very thirsty, and not a little disgusted by the conviction that our shooting ardour had been taken advantage of by the villagers of Condivettam, for the purpose of destroying a "rogue" elephant that possibly had been amongst them for years, and which they had not the means of destroying themselves. To our great comfort, we found that a plentiful supply of milk had been procured by our indefatigable old Apoo; indeed, we had in abundance every requisite for the important occupation of eating and drinking, except drinking vessels, and these by some mistake had been omitted: our stock consisted of one huge tumbler, which from its invaluable inexhaustible qualities was called the "big drink," holding something under a gallon, and a pewter salt-cellar. This deficiency obliged us to have recourse to some rather ludicrous shifts. Mrs. Gamp, from "motives of delicacy," drank her spirits out of the teapot; we frequently did likewise, necessity being our excuse; and many a laugh was raised when we pledged one another, one out of the spout of a teapot, the other out of the salt-cellar.

We had scarcely laid ourselves down in a recumbent position, which the excitement of the "rogue," the excessive heat of the day, and the previously sleepless night rendered most congenial to our wishes, when in rushed some more trackers, bursting with the intelligence that there was a herd within a mile or so. Duff examined the men this time, and their story appearing credible, we started again in the direction pointed out. We left our horses in the bed of the river, and hurried on foot up another river. I was much struck with the eagerness of the young Moorman, who had discovered the herd, and hoped to reap the reward: he kept continually taking up handfuls of sand and scattering it, that we might not lose a chance of giving them the wind. When we reached the spot indicated, the herd had vanished; but an enormous "rogue" occupied the centre of a small patna, or field, of some four or five acres. We had advanced most stealthily, and were considering how to circumvent him, when he scented us, and, without looking our way, rolled off to the jungle in majestic, but scarcely graceful style, and at a pace that forbade all pursuit. An elephant's ordinary pace, which strikes one as being quite slow, is in reality about six or seven knots, and that amongst high matted jungle-grass, rendering a pursuit little better than a labour in vain. We might have fired a shot at his stern, but it would not have killed him, and it is very improbable that it would have had any other effect than that of hastening his departure; moreover, we still hoped we were in the vicinity of the herd. That they had been there was quite evident from their very recent spoor; but elephants are so very lively and excited after their mid-day siesta, that it is almost impossible to approach them. We tracked on for miles through the jungle, every now and then flattering ourselves that we were drawing near the objects of our pursuit. We passed several ruined tanks; in crossing one, we saw a large herd of pigs, and had a severe race in trying to cut them off; but they were too quick for us. However, thinking we were far away from any elephants, we gave them a volley, when, to our disgust, an elephant, which we had not seen standing at the edge of the jungle, dashed in and disappeared; had we seen him sooner, we might probably have secured him. At sunset we finished at a ruined tank, where the deer, and hog, and peacock were just assembling in scores, and returned to camp rather beat. The mosquitos were very numerous, but we had taken better precautions against their attacks.

On getting up in the morning, I found an unexpected bedfellow, and not a very agreeable one, in the shape of a small scorpion. How he had introduced himself I cannot say; but he doubtless passed a warmer and more comfortable night than I should have, had I been aware of his proximity. I once tried the experiment of the scorpion girt by fire, so poetically described by Byron; but I cannot think a jury of scorpions would bring in a verdict of *felo de se.* It appears to me that the animal stings itself in its agony, but without premeditation.

In the morning I attended the lesson of the young elephant I have already mentioned. He was very obstinate, but succumbed to persuasion when force was quite useless. He was very hungry, having been nearly starved for several days, though the affected deliberation with which he took the grass offered to him was really amusing,—like a spoilt child who has been crying for a bun, and then, when he gets it, pretends not to want it in the least.

CHAPTER XVII.

RUINED TANKS—THOUGHTS ON CIVILIZATION—REMARKABLE RUINS—PEA-FOWL—APOO—RED KITE.

NOT finding that the sport at Condivettam equalled our anticipations, we started about mid-day for another jungle, distant some eight or ten miles. The first five miles lay down stream, and I think it was one of the hottest and most fatiguing marches I ever remember. The sand was so loose, that we sank to the ankles at every step, and the glare and refraction equalled that of Egypt's most burning plains. The fatigue of the coolies was most painful to witness, more especially as several had sickened with fever and dysentery, and were very weak; one in particular was dangerously ill.

After leaving the river, our route skirted several ruined tanks, some of very large size, seven or eight miles in circumference. I suppose there is no country in the world, of equal size, which can show so many remains of works of irrigation and past civilization as Ceylon. Cingalese historians affirm that there were formerly 200,000 artificial tanks in the island. I should say 20,000, or even 2,000, would be nearer the truth. Many of them are as large as the most magnificent ones in India. Mantotte is sixteen or eighteen miles in extent, and Minere is even larger. When one takes into consideration the immense size of the stones, and the long distances whence they must have been transported, through districts now impassable from jungle, the amount of labour visible in these tanks is really very astonishing. The stones are fashioned with chisel and wedge as at present, although the natives affirm that they are 1,500 years old; however, all dates in Ceylon are most indefinite. They say there were giants in those days, and that the works now visible, and astonishing the traveller, are those of a race of men forty feet high. The natives particularly assert that no elephants were employed in their construction.

Some curious thoughts strike one in passing these remains of former prosperity and population; we see in them, not the remains of a people who though conquered still exist, but of a race that has been entirely swept away from the face of the earth. Ceylon, formerly with a population of five or six millions, and supplying the whole of the Coromandel coast and other parts of India with rice, has now scarcely a population of forty mouths to the square mile, and even these, but for the supplies of grain from the Malabar coast, would starve. As it is quite possible that our little planet has almost accomplished its brief span in the cycle of eternity, and that soon it will, by one of those convulsions that are daily taking place, and apparent even to our limited vision, in the immensity of space, drop from its orbit, be burnt up by a comet, change the angle of its axis, or commit some other vagary that will render it uninhabitable by human beings with lungs and atmospheric necessities, we ought properly to be approaching that state in which we are led to expect the "lion will lie down with the lamb," and the earth, thoroughly peopled and civilized, will contain but one universal faith. It is very startling, then, to find that to all appearance the world is just as far removed from this state of universal excellence and civilization, as in the earliest days of which we have any notice; it would seem as if civilization were a constant quantity, neither increasing nor diminishing, but only changing the sphere of its influence. It appears to ebb and flow with much the same regularity as the tides of the ocean: if it is high tide in one quarter of the globe, it is low in the other. There is an old French proverb, which remarks that vice is also a constant quantity, and never varies; "*Moins il y a de fripons aux galères, plus il y en a dehors,*" and *vice versâ*.

The glory of the East, of Babylon, Jerusalem, Egypt, Tyre, Greece, and Rome, has departed, and we can hardly assert that the blank is more than supplied by the civilization of the western portion of Europe, and the continent of America. But even the civilization of that New World seems to nave prospered and arisen on the ruins of polished and refined nations, of whom we have not even the most remote conception or tradition. The ruins of Mexico and Yucatan, of Peru and Ohio, prove beyond a doubt, that whatever may have been the state of those countries when discovered by Europeans, and whatever may be the amount of ignorance and degradation which now envelops some of them, yet they were at one time inhabited by nations at least as enlightened as some of the present kingdoms of Europe.

Many of the ruins of Ceylon are very remarkable, and on the grandest scale. The city of Anurajahpoorah, which I before had occasion to mention, contained a palace with 1,600 columns, of fine marble and elaborate workmanship; a temple composed of 366 pagodas, twenty-four of great size, some 270 feet in height, made of solid brickwork, and once entirely covered with chunam, or lime formed of oyster-shells, which, when properly prepared, takes as good a polish, and is almost as durable, as marble.

The number of pea-fowl we saw on this day's march, and, in fact, throughout the whole trip, was something incredible. A flock of peacocks is at any time, or in any place, a very fine sight; but at sunrise and sunset, when the rays of the rising or setting sun fall obliquely on their gorgeous plumage, the effect is very grand. Alexander's delight at the first sight of peacocks, as eloquently described by Ælian, was so great, that he forbade his soldiers to destroy them, on pain of death. At Athens they were valued at 1,000 drachms (32*l.*) the pair; and in Rome, the breeding of them attained as much importance, and was as much cared for, as that of Cochin Chinas in these days. In Ceylon, they are not without their use; inasmuch as the number of snakes, large and small, they destroy is very great. Their chief food, however, consists in ants, and I doubt whether even the Great Ant Lion himself manages to consume as many as a full-grown Peacock.

We had left the country of the Cingalese, and all the scattered inhabitants of the districts we now passed through were Moormen or Tamuls.

The country this season was more unhealthy than had ever been known, and all the natives we met, gave lamentable accounts of the amount of sickness in their villages; some of them were almost depopulated.

We had some Ibis for dinner, much the same as the Sacred Ibis of Egypt, and most delicious eating; we had now also arrived in the region of milk, a great luxury, as the water everywhere was so utterly beastly, that it was quite impossible to luxuriate in that delicious "*drinky for drinky*," that good liquor would have enabled one to enjoy. However, whether there was milk or not, we lived in the most luxurious style; a satisfactory part of the arrangements, for which we were entirely indebted to our old Apoo, or *chef-de-cuisine*. He was a perfect character in his way, and for an extended pic-nic party like ours, invaluable. His exterior was about as ludicrous and unprepossessing as that of any old party of something under sixty I have ever seen. His nose resembled the elongated organ that is generally represented in the pictures of a certain dark gentleman, who shall be nameless, when he is being drawn out by the tongs of the good Saint Dunstan. His mouth occupied more than half his physiognomy, and its cavernous dimensions were fearfully increased by the total absence of all teeth. His dress was in keeping with his figure and features. It consisted of a white night-cap, or a blue bird's-eye, wound round the head; a very slang shooting-coat, the present of some former master, without shirt or waistcoat, and a petticoat, or comboy, for continuations.

The different fashions of wearing these "comboys" are almost innumerable; at one time they are worn as a regular petticoat, down to the ankles; at another, as a kind of pantaloon drawn tight up between the legs; the next time you meet the proprietor, you find it wrapped round his loins like a girdle, or round his head as a turban; it serves as a sheet by night, and a cloak by day; it is alternately a towel and a table-cloth; in fact, a Scotch plaid is a joke to it.

The Apoo was the best caterer I ever met, and most unhesitating as to the means he took to replenish his commissariat: when the Cingalese refused to sell milk or chickens, he not only milked the cows, but he used to borrow a gun and shoot the chickens, knowing perfectly well that when they were dead, the natives would be happy enough to let us have them: it was certainly what you might term sharp practice, but I do not know that under the circumstances, it was not excusable. Provisions were generally refused, merely because we were English, and as such not very popular; we might forage in vain for chickens, rice, and milk, whilst a party of

Moormen coming after us, would, at something under one-sixth of the price we had offered, fill themselves with all manner of good things.

The time consumed between the death of gentlemen or lady chickens, and their appearance at table is very short; they are generally presented in the form of a de-spatch cock or chicken, cooked before it has had time to get cold. It is no unusual thing for the cock that greets you in the yard on your arrival at a rest-house, to welcome you again in another shape on the table when you have washed your hands.

The Cingalese have a remarkable dislike to parting with their chickens for the purposes of food; the reason is, they not unfrequently imagine they are tenanted by deceased parents or relations: an affectionate son or mother, therefore, might for a few annas, be unwittingly disposing of the earthly tenement of a parent or child.

The old Apoo having once discovered *our*, or rather I believe I ought to say *my* weakness for milk, exerted himself most energetically and imperatively in his endeavours to procure it.—"Well Apoo, milk got?" "Yes, sar, plenty milk come, plenty fowl got," was the usual greeting on our return to camp. He played me once a practical joke on the subject of milk; it was a mild one certainly, but afforded him an immensity of amusement, and he chuckled and crackled his toothless old jaws, till I thought some part of his high-dried carcase would have given way. I teased him one day good humouredly about not getting so much milk as he might, and told him to be sure and have some that night; he nodded assent, but said nothing. In the evening when we had camped, and were sitting like Patriarchs or Shepherd Kings at the tent door, the old Apoo came up grinning, and said, "Master, milk come," at the same time introducing two natives bearing a gallon or two of milk. In a few minutes he appeared again, "Master, more milk come," and showed us more gallons. This went on four or five times, till we had milk enough to have drowned the party. I fancy it was the first practical joke the old man had ever played, and certainly he enjoyed it.

There were a great quantity of tortoises or land turtle in the bed, and on the banks of the river where we camped, and the coolies brought them to us in numbers; one species is good to eat, and our respected old friend made some very tolerable soup from them. There were also a great many Brahminy or red kite, a Sawmy bird that is worshipped and never destroyed by the natives. This kite is a great enemy of the tortoise; they cannot break the shell of the latter with their beaks, but they carry them up in their claws to a great height, and then dash them on some stone or rock. It is said they display very acute instinct, approaching to reason, in their choice of rocks, and in the way they take shots; sometimes, however, they make mistakes, as Euripides found to his cost, when his bald head, like that of Chaucer's monk, "shining like any glass," was mistaken by the kite for a white stone, and the tortoise let fall in consequence, destroying at once the meditation and the existence of the venerable poet.

This bird is also a great destroyer of serpents; and it is doubtless owing to the united efforts of the peacocks and the kites, that reptiles do not multiply even more than at present. It is asserted by the natives, that the Brahminy kite will not attack the cobra: they say that formerly he always devoured them, but that in consequence of the cobra's successful appearance in the character of the good Samaritan, shading Guatama when ill and asleep, from the rays of the sun, with his hood, he got into favour with that deity: and that one day having lost, I imagine, some near relation by means of the kite, he addressed his humble petition to the god, saying (he spoke with the Yankee idiom and drawl), "That that thar everlasting kite was death upon snakes, and no mistake; and that if Sawmy did not protect him, why he must give up." Sawmy on the spot granted his prayer, and immediately put the spectacles on his hood, the sight of which deters the kite, however hungry, from regaling himself on the cobra or his friends.

The coolies were sickening fast; and, notwithstanding a most liberal allowance of castor oil, and opium, chalk and ginger, one poor fellow seemed getting worse, and his state was anything but satisfactory. We had some strong soup made of the turtle for him, but he refused to take it on account of his caste. We insisted on his doing so, calling it physic; but he would not swallow it, returning it from his mouth almost immediately.

CHAPTER XVIII.

ELEPHANT SHOOTING.

During the night the elephants were roaring and the peacocks crying; the latter noise somewhat resembling the cry of a pack of wolves.

We had sent trackers out over night, and having heard the elephants comparatively near, we were very sanguine as to finding them, so we gobbled up our breakfast as quickly as possible, and prepared our fire-arms. We had just completed our labours, and were soothing our impatience with the calumet of peace, when in came the trackers, and reported a herd close at hand. We were off immediately, and after riding for about two miles down the stream, dismounted, and entered the jungle.

The etiquette of elephant shooting is very strict, and the necessity of its observance quite palpable, for where three or four sportsmen and twenty or thirty natives are all eager and excited, confusion and accident would inevitably occur but for some preconcerted understanding or arrangement. At the beginning of a campaign lots are drawn for the first shot, and the others follow in succession; the man who is first one day being last the next, and working up till his turn comes again. It happened to be my first shot, so when we approached the jungle where the animals were supposed to be, I went to the front, and followed close in the footsteps of the leading tracker.

The stealthy way in which the natives creep through jungle is astonishing: I am not a very heavy party, but I felt myself more like a young elephant following a fawn than anything else. I was so intent upon following my guide as quietly and as quickly as I could, that I did not perceive my companions had stayed behind, till at the end of ten or twelve minutes, I found myself alone with the tracker. His dress, although well adapted for running away from the game, was scarcely elegant; his head was closely shaven, and his copper-coloured skin utterly divested of all covering, but that of the smallest of all cloths about his waist. He imitated the various cries of elephants, peacocks, and other wild denizens of the forest, in order to attract the attention of my companions, but in vain; so we proceeded on our course alone. After we had tracked about ten minutes longer, the Moorman suddenly stopped, as if shot, and pointed me out a huge mass at a distance of about sixty yards, which I could not at first quite distinguish as an elephant: however, on creeping nearer, I made out my friend; he was standing with his back towards me, fanning himself with his long ears. It is not always wise to attack an elephant quite alone, especially when you cannot depend upon your gun-carrier remaining by you in extremity. From this man's bumptious, swaggering manner when in camp, and from his having displayed unmistakable symptoms of alarm when engaged with the "rogue" some days before, I felt convinced that "my pretty gentleman," as the gipsies say, would run at the slightest appearance of danger. However, I had not much time to consider, for the elephant turned lazily round, and commenced moving in my direction. This was a great deal too tempting to be resisted, so, following the bent of my inclination, I advanced to meet him; he did not see me, I think, till I was about six yards from him, when he stopped and prepared to turn, — rather a long business sometimes with individuals of his species. I immediately gave him a shot in the centre of the forehead, about three inches above the root of the trunk. The effect was instantaneous; he subsided like a great hayrick, without a groan or a struggle of any kind, falling exactly in the position he was standing, with one leg advanced, in the act of turning. I had never seen an animal die so immediately, and I felt almost startled at witnessing the power of one small ounce of lead in destroying so effectually the vitality of such a huge mass.

My tracker, who had retreated as I advanced, now came up, and while he was engaged in securing the tail—the only thing a sportsman has to show for his danger and trouble—I was contemplating my handiwork, really more than half sorry for what I had done, and more than half ashamed of having destroyed one of the most sagacious of God's creatures, without any object whatever but that of saying I *had* done so. I had, indeed, half resolved to return to camp and not wantonly commit any more murder, when suddenly I heard the jungle crashing quite close at hand, and had just time to turn, when I met another elephant "mooning" right up to where his deceased friend was being deprived of his caudal honours; he had evidently heard the shot, and was now about to fall a victim to his curiosity. All my humane regrets, philelephantine sentiments, I am ashamed to say, vanished in a second, and I advanced to meet him with much more excitement than I did the first. He did not see me till I was quite close, when he stopped short, and, without showing any desire to retire, eyed me in rather a fierce manner, at the same time lifting his trunk, as if implying that he *could*, if he *chose*, "chaw me up in considerable less than no time." Expecting a charge, I glanced round to look for my second gun, but my friend the tracker had disappeared: he seemed to regard elephants much in the same style as Ulysses was advised to regard Circe—

> "O fly her rage, thy conquest is thy flight;"

and he certainly acted on that advice, for he vanished whenever an elephant showed any pugnacious symptoms, and always returned sprightly and elated when the danger was passed, as if he were himself a victor.

My guncarrier having disappeared, I was left in the agreeable position of standing face to face with an elephant in anything but an amiable mood, with only one shot to rely upon. I ought properly to have retired, as attacking an elephant single-handed with only one barrel is too dangerous an amusement to be often attempted with success. My first impulse on perceiving the failure of my second gun was to retire from the scene of action; but then I thought of the tail, and determined to fire first, and trust to being able to accomplish a retreat afterwards, if necessary. All this passed in one second, and as the elephant at that moment gave a shrill trumpet, a sign either of rage or fear (in this instance I think it was the latter), I found there was no time to lose; so I hurried up to within ten yards of his head, when, just as he was going to charge or retire, I cannot say which, I shot him in the forehead, in the identical spot I had struck the other. His death was quite as instantaneous as that of his lady companion, and, poor brute, whether his intention had been friendly or hostile did not much signify, for he was cut off in the flower of his youth, and pride of his strength, by a comparative pigmy, whom, had he been conscious of his power, he might have destroyed and crumpled up with far greater ease even than Mr. Cobden could the empire of Russia.

I had now, as a beginner, had the singular good fortune to kill two elephants, I might almost say right and left, without any assistance, and with about as much danger to myself as there would be in shooting a fat ox in Smithfield market. I was quite satisfied with my exploit, and being joined by my tracker, who had only run far enough to be out of any possible reach of danger to himself, and of any possible service to me, I sat down on the victim of my destructive propensities, and lighted the cheroot of contemplation, intending to wait till my companions found us out, or till the tracker discovered them. My attendant had been hacking away at the tail, and I had been puffing at the weed for some few minutes, when suddenly we heard a crashing in the jungle, at the distance of about a hundred yards or so. Quite elated with my former success, which a few minutes before I had had no desire to increase, I now felt it would be incomplete without following the fresh game that was afoot; so seizing the empty gun, I made signs to the Moorman for the powder-horn, but to my disgust found it had been left with my other gun carrier. The loaded gun was soon shouldered, and, followed closely by the Moorman with the empty one, I rushed off in the direction of the crash. I had gone about a hundred yards, when I caught a glimpse of an old she elephant, with a punchy or young one between her legs, hurrying off at a good pace. I went after her as fast as I could, but the jungle had suddenly become very bad, and I found I was gaining but little upon her, when, after about five minutes, she "*yawed*" slightly in her course, which gave me the opportunity of making a short cut, and getting in front of her shoulder; I fired at the distance of thirty yards, but she was going too fast, and I was too much blown, to make an effectual investment of powder and lead. The ball however struck her on the head, and had the effect of stopping her immediately; she faced round, and I hurried up till within twelve yards, when I gave her the remaining barrel. This staggered her, and almost brought her to her knees; for a second I thought she was falling, but suddenly collecting herself, and trumpeting fiercely with rage and agony, she charged upon me. My position was, in truth, now anything but agreeable. I was quite alone, the Moorman having rushed shouting away immediately he discovered the failure of the first shot, within fifteen yards of an enraged mamma elephant, with an empty gun, and a close intricate jungle all around, and no apparent chance of any diversion in my favour. I did not, however, take any time to consider my situation, but retreated as fast as my legs could carry me, and dived through bush and brake and round impervious thickets, with an agility that afterwards astonished me. Had I been a hero, I should now probably, like Alexander, when he met King Porus mounted on his elephants, and attended by his legions on the banks of the Hydaspes, have congratulated myself on having at length "encountered a danger suitable to the greatness of my soul," but I suppose I am no hero, for my thoughts were anything but congratulatory, and I thought far more of retiring as speedily as possible, than of facing the danger unmoved. Unfortunately, there was not a single tree of sufficient size to afford me any protection; but, nevertheless, the closeness of the jungle, although it entangled and embarrassed me, whereas it was as dry sticks to the elephant, had the advantage of preventing her keeping her eye fixed upon me. I had retired in this manner about two hundred yards, though it appeared nearly two miles, hearing the elephant crashing behind me, when to my delight I saw a respectable sized tree, with a stump and a bush rope, offering the most convenient means of ascent. I rushed to it, and ascended with an agility that could not have failed to be highly satisfactory to any of my friends who had witnessed it, and would have raised the envy of an ordinary uran-utan. I had attained a height of about twenty feet, to the utter annihilation of my habiliments, particularly the unmentionables, when I heard the elephant approaching, this time much slower. She passed within six yards of the tree, where, like King Charles, I was concealed; and had she been of an inquiring turn of mind, and looked up, she could not have failed to see me. Elephants seldom, if ever, hunt by scent, but their hearing is so acute, as almost to answer the same purpose; and I fancy she had followed my tortuous course by that sense. Her appearance as she passed my perch, was not certainly such as to make me regret having escaped her. She was bleeding from two shots in the head, and her eyes were actually starting out of her head with rage. She carried her extremities, tail and trunk, both erect, and she certainly did not at that moment present a favourable example of—

> "That wisest of brutes, with gentle might adorn'd,
> Though powerful, not destructive;"

for she looked as decidedly truculent and unamiable as any four-legged animal could do. However, she was perfectly right to pursue and kill, if possible, those who hunt, torture, and destroy her race, merely for the sake of sport. If I was an elephant, I should have very little compunction in flattening any European sportsman I could meet with.

It was not till I had descended from my retreat, that I was aware of the actual danger I had escaped. The tree was entirely hollowed out and consumed by the white ant, and nothing but the shell remained. Had I been a stone or two heavier, it is probable it would not have borne me, and, as it was, if the elephant had seen me, and pulled at the tree, it would have crumbled down like so much paper.

When she had retired, and I could hear no more of her, I descended, and sitting at the bottom of the tree, proceeded to relight the cheroot, whose soothing effect was so much required to reestablish my shaken equanimity. After a few minutes,

I heard the Moorman calling, and on my answering him, he soon reached the spot, and as far as I could understand his signs, expressed his astonishment at seeing me in the usual form of the human species: he had expected, I fancy, to have found me in a somewhat flattened and elongated shape. I really had great cause to be thankful that I had escaped so well. It is always dangerous to attack a female with young; and alone, with no second gun, and in a bad jungle, I had no reason to expect I should have escaped as well as I did.

The females of all animals with young are savage, and mamma elephants are especially so (though I have certainly seen some remarkable cases of maternal selfishness and *insouciance* even in the elephant); they generally show fight, and display more activity and acuteness than even an old "rogue." The troops of Pyrrhus, at the battle of Heraclea, were entirely routed by an old female rushing to the assistance of her punchy, whom she heard in difficulties.

In this instance I might have retired without loss of honour; and, in fact, caution would have prompted me to do so, but I believe when the bumps were being served out, I happened to be absent when that particular bump was being distributed, and somebody else got my share: I shrewdly suspect it must have been my friend the

Moorman. Moreover, there was no tutelary deity to whisper in my ear the very sensible advice the goddess of Love vouchsafed to Adonis, when starting on his last Shikar expedition:—

> "To furious animals advance not nigh;
> Fly those that follow; follow those that fly."

So, as many men do, when acting under strong excitement, I embarked in an undertaking on the impulse of the moment, which I was only too happy to have an opportunity of repenting of at leisure. I thought of nothing but securing the tail, and forgot the danger till almost too late.

My tracker and myself now proceeded to return to camp; but, in about a quarter of an hour, we heard our companions shouting, and soon found our way towards them. There had been a large herd afoot, and they had seen several elephants, and shot three.

As we were returning home through the jungle, we came upon more elephants, in a very thick patch of jungle. Duff killed one, in first-rate style, before any other of the party had caught sight of them. She was a female, and a very fair specimen of her sex, standing rather over nine feet at the shoulder, which would make her upwards of ten feet on the top of the back.

We returned to camp well satisfied with a very good afternoon's amusement. My idea of the sport, from that day's experience was, that in ordinary cases it was one of two extremes—either too tame to afford the necessary amount of excitement, or too dangerous to leave much room for agreeable sensations. The shooting is very difficult, and requires the sportsman to be almost as quick a snap shot as if firing at snipe. Of course, when the elephant stands till you take a deliberate potshot at his head at short pistol range, anybody who does not shut his eyes when firing, may make certain of killing; but in thick jungle, when he is moving rapidly about, and only exposing the vulnerable parts of his body for a second or two at a time, the hunter must be as quick as lightning. Elephant and snipe-shooting illustrate the old adage, that extremes frequently meet. In the former case you slay an enormous animal with an incredibly small piece of lead; in the latter, you destroy a minute bird with an expenditure of powder and lead equally disproportioned; and in both cases it is snapshooting, and the one depends almost as much on practice as the other.

The nature of the wound in the last elephant D. shot, displayed in a remarkable manner the soft porous nature of the animal's cranium. The shot entered behind the ear, and we could feel the ball within an inch of the skin in the forehead, and with a knife cut it out at once. The bullet had penetrated the whole region of the enormous head. The facial line of the elephant, that is, the vertical height of skull compared with its horizontal length, is very elevated, and to phrenologists gives the appearance of wisdom. The ancients, especially the Greeks, and from them the Romans, attached the greatest importance to the shape and elevation of the head, and attributed the highest intellectual qualities to the elephant; and on several antique medals, the head of Socrates is found united with that of an elephant. Amongst the Hindoos, Ganesea, the god of wisdom, is represented with a human body and an elephant's head. The owl also owes its reputation for wisdom to the shape of its head; but both it and the elephant possess a very small modicum of brain; but that is no criterion of wisdom, for, as I before remarked, the bee, with the highest intellectual and reasoning organs, has no brain at all; and the woodcock, notoriously the least sagacious of birds, has the largest proportionate development of brain.

The elephants were roaring in numbers during the night, in the direction of those we had shot, but though we hunted early and late, we saw no sign of them.

CHAPTER XIX.

MALIENTEE—PEACOCKS—INSECT LIFE—MISTAKEN SHOT—NIGHTS IN CEYLON—MONOTONY OF SEASONS.

On the 23d we moved camp to a tank, called Malientee, at the edge of a splendid forest, differing from most of the Ceylon forests, in having fine open glades and avenues, formed by magnificent trees, under which we could see for a considerable distance. The camp was one of the most picturesque we had yet made, and the excessive beauty of the evening sunset, and the astonishing clearness of the atmosphere, rendered the short twilight most delicious, reminding one of an English summer's evening.

Just before sunset, the peacocks began to assemble on the edge of the forest, preparatory to their evening gleaning in the paddy fields; they were superb fellows, with tails of an immense length and spread; they kept assembling by twos and threes, flying in with loud cackles, much as you see pheasants collecting for their evening feed, in the immediate neighbourhood of a good preserve in England. They were, moreover, quite as plentiful; we counted at one time as many as forty, and there were scores we could not see. Several herds of pig and deer also visited the paddy fields; the former, bolder than either the pea-fowl or the deer, came well to the front. The scene altogether, with the bright rays of the setting sun glancing on the magnificent trees, the white tents, and the coolies and natives in picturesque groups, cooking their rice round small fires, with the wild inhabitants of the forest, feeding and frolicking in unsuspicious enjoyment in the back ground, formed as perfect a picture of tropical scenery as one could well imagine.

Tantalising as this quantity of game was, we resisted the temptation of firing, lest we should frighten away the nobler game. We had an interview with some of the best trackers of the place, friends of Duff's, and after agreeing for the price to be paid for the discovery of a herd, (I believe some four or five rupees,) we despatched them to the jungle, and retired to our tents.

Elephants were roaring and trumpeting in all directions, some within a quarter of a mile of the camp, and about 6 A.M. a long tracker, of most remarkable anatomical structure, who reminded me much of the description and pictures of "Le Gros Serpent" in the "Last of the Mohicans," came in to announce the discovery of a herd. We were off at once, but on arriving at the jungle specified, we discovered they had somehow taken alarm and vanished; we tracked them for several hours, and it was quite wonderful to observe the sagacity of our trackers; any little twig that sprang up as we passed, any turned leaf, the slightest mud on the trees or the bushes, was enough to guide them on the trail, at a round pace of three miles an hour. However, the ground was as hard as baked clay, and as the elephants increased their distance from us, all the guiding marks I have mentioned disappeared, and we had no signs whatever to direct us.

Amongst the wonderful forms assumed by insect life in Ceylon, is one exactly resembling a twig. It takes the exact colour of the tree on which it lives, and you may watch and examine it for half an hour, before you can quite convince yourself that it is an insect, and not a vegetable substance. The power of assuming the colour of the soil, and the trees amongst which they dwell, is possessed by numerous animals and insects in the tropics, and indeed in all parts of the world. Many of the snakes and lizards are quite undistinguishable from the trees and shrubs they frequent. The elephant is also a remarkable instance of this; its colour is so exactly that of the trees and of the rocks amongst which it roams, that more than once I have known an elephant was within a few yards of me, and have tried in vain to distinguish it from the surrounding trunks and rocks.

After our unsuccessful hunt we returned to camp, and having had warm thirsty work, and knowing that milk was plenty in camp, we had a sort of scurry race home. The ground was as hard as possible, and was poached with old elephant and buffalo spoor, and the paddy fields were full of fissures, broad enough to have broken all four legs of a horse at once. To avoid this uneven ground, I turned Punchy on to a bank about four feet high and about two feet broad, which separated one paddy field from another. We had galloped in safety for some three or four hundred yards, and were distancing our competitors, and the vision of an ocean of milk in the "Big drink" was gratefully distinct, when the spirit of mischief in my steed outweighed all his sense of caution and respect, either for his master's limbs or his own, for in full career he suddenly began curveting and springing from side to side, and of course quicker than I can relate it, he missed his footing, and we rolled off on to the iron ground with anything but a pleasing crash: the shock was a severe one, but strange to say, we received no greater damage than a few bruises and a broken saddle. Punchy, who had rolled completely over me, recovered himself before his master, and jumping up, galloped off with head and tail erect, turning his head from side to side, and I am convinced, if ever a horse did laugh, grinning heartily at my misfortune.

This was not our only mishap, for close to camp another of the party fired at what he thought was a jackal sneaking in the grass. He made a remarkably pretty shot with his rifle, and knocked the animal over; but on going up to it, he found, to his intense annoyance, it was one of the Pariah dogs, that

> "Shaggy, and lean, and shrewd, with pointed ears,
> And tail cropped short, half lurcher and half cur,"

frequent in numbers the native villages.

Next morning, as we were enjoying the matutinal cheroot, and watching the artful manœuvres of Punchy to extend his halter, and have a playful nip at his horsekeeper, who was sleeping near him, the owner of the deceased dog came up and with most piteous lamentations bewailed his loss, and appealed to our sympathy and generosity. The peasant with his dead ass in the "Sentimental Journey" did not present half so touching a spectacle. The assistance of the Apoo was called in to translate our petitioner's account of his dog. The deceased animal must indeed have been "semi-homo canis:" there was nothing, from pulling down an elephant to slaying a bear, from catching snakes to driving home the cows, that this wonderful animal did not perform every day; and if he had been the famous dog "Soter" himself, the sole survivor of those forty dogs who, superior to their canine brethren of Rome, saved the city of Corinth, his loss could not have caused more apparent distress. The adage of "give a dog a bad name and hang him," was apparently reversed in this case, and a new version of "shoot a dog, and all the canine excellences will attach themselves to him in æternitatem," established. After an animated discussion with the bereaved, and, by his account, ruined proprietor of the murdered dog, we commenced a negotiation regarding the amount of blood-money expected, when we found that the sum of half a rupee, or one shilling, satisfied his most exorbitant demands; and that for a like sum half the neighbouring village were ready to sacrifice their affection to their interests.

At 3 P.M. we were off again to track elephants. We worked hard till dark, and saw plenty of fresh signs, but no elephants. The scenery was most beautiful, and the trees finer than any I had yet seen. At a short distance, the clumps of isolated trees resembled oaks and elm. You might at any time fancy yourself in a gentleman's park; and it was literally only when you were startled by the roar of an elephant in the distant forest, or the crash of a flock of monkeys, as they sprang chattering away, and saw the flocks of pea-fowl and hog and wild buffalo, that you were reminded that the torrid, and not the temperate zone, was at that moment the scene of your enjoyment.

The nights in Ceylon are invariably oppressive; and though the sky is cloudless, and the stars shine out clear and twinkling, the restless, perspiring European, tossing from side to side, covets in vain the bracing luxury of an English night,—one of those invigorating starlights that caused the exulting exclamation of that practical sovereign, Frederick the Great: "Voici un temps qui vaudra bien des soldats à la Prusse." But the evenings, as I before remarked, are exquisitely beautiful, and delicious in the extreme, and the most fastidious climacterian could devise nothing more enjoyable. When sheltered from the fierce rays of the sun by the matted forests, even midday is perfectly endurable; and I often fancied that, with a parrot and a gun, and a male—though I should prefer a female—Friday I could, like Robinson Crusoe, manage to exist with considerable enjoyment of life.

But there is a monotony in the seasons that becomes tiresome: it is *always summer*, the only change being from wet to dry. For six months, or rather nine months, it is a rainless, for the other three a drenching summer. There is no autumn, no winter; and that most delicious spring-time, when one fancies the Divine Creator grants new leases, and imparts fresh life and vigour to all the works and creatures of His hand; when birds and beasts, men and plants, seem striving to make the most of their appointed season; when every day, nay, almost every hour, sees the buttercup or the primrose, the violet or the bluebell, springing up, and re-decking their accustomed haunts; "when the time of the singing bird is come, and the voice of the turtle is heard in our land;" when the days are too short for the nest-building of the thrush, and the honey-gathering of the bee, for the poor man's toil, and for the rich man's enjoyment; when the young salmon dashes joyously to the sea, and the old salmon betakes himself, fat and silvery, to the rivers, &c. &c. &c. and all that sort of thing (sentiment does not operate beneficially in these days, unless applied in very strong doses), is entirely wanting in Ceylon. *Toujours perdrix* is a nuisance, and continual summer is one also.

During the night the elephants were heard

quite close to camp, some having been in the paddy field just at hand. They sometimes collect in numbers round any of their dead companions, and roar and tear up the ground and trees much as cows or oxen will do on the scene of bloodshed in England. Duff told me that, some years before, he had shot an old dam, but the young one had escaped, and in the night it began calling for its dead mother; its cries were soon answered by other elephants approaching from different points, till the whole forest seemed alive with herds roaring and answering each other: he was convinced there must have been upwards of a hundred elephants in their vicinity that night; and he described the effect of their fearful concert as being most startling, and almost unearthly. Next morning not one was to be seen.

At half-past 5 A.M. off with trackers to a jungle, where elephants had been discovered during the night. We managed to approach them in very tolerable order, and Duff, whose first shot it was, bagged one in first-rate style; the others broke, and scattered through the forest. One was badly wounded, and we followed him for several miles by the blood: poor brute, it must have bled fearfully.

After a sharp pursuit of about an hour, we came up with him in a thick impenetrable jungle, where only the practised eyes of the natives could distinguish him. "First turn" tried to get his shot, but could not see; in the meantime the animal broke away, and distanced us. Elephants, even when desperately wounded, are seldom or ever found dead afterwards; and the natives affirm that they have never discovered an elephant whose death they could not immediately account for. It is said that a wound in the trunk is mortal; and the sagacious brute, knowing this, lifts it up as far as he can out of harm's way, when charging, or approaching danger.

One of the trackers, during our pursuit of the wounded elephant, killed a very dangerous snake, which was lying coiled up under a tree, enjoying its midday siesta. The natives say that cobras and tic-polongas will destroy elephants with their venom. They can easily pierce the skin, either in the tip of the trunk, which is almost as thin and tender as an infant's, or in the heel. "Dan shall be a serpent by the way, an adder in the path, that biteth the horses' heels, so that his rider falls backward," would imply that horses might be struck in the same manner, and certainly their dread of snakes is very great.

Off at two o'clock, in a desperate hurry after a herd, reported close at hand. We had tracked some two hours, when we came suddenly upon as grand a grouping of wild Eastern forest nature as it is possible to imagine. We entered a patna, or open space of twenty acres or so in extent, and at the extreme end of it were collected a herd of about thirty or forty elephants, lazily flapping their long ears, and pulling the branches from the neighbouring jungle; (the trackers counted thirty outside the forest, and asserted that, from the movement of the trees, there must have been twenty or thirty more inside.) Some were lying down, with their heads resting between their fore-legs: it is curious that, when elephants were first introduced into England in 1567, it was believed that the "olifawnte that boweth not the knees," actually had not the power of bending its leg. It certainly was a very grand sight, and alone fully repaid one for all the trouble and heat we had endured. We studied the direction of the wind, and approached with the greatest care; but, like large herds of anything else, they were very *skeary,* and got away into the jungle before we could secure more than one.

I had again followed my friend the long tracker, and as my companions entered the jungle to the right, I, at a signal from him, dashed in to the left. Had I been half a minute sooner, I should have had an excellent chance; but, unfortunately, there was a kind of nullah, or ravine, with some four feet of water to be crossed, and as I was in the middle of this, with the water up to my armpits, and my feet stuck fast in the mud, five or six elephants crossed the nullah about twenty yards from me. If I had been on *terra firma*, I might certainly have "realized" a tail; but in the uncertain position I then occupied, not knowing how deep I was to sink in the mud, and having no fancy to tempt a charge in that situation, I made the best of my way across in the direction they were taking. They got about thirty or forty yards' start of me on landing, and "sloped" away through the jungle at a great pace. I ran after one old gentleman, till I really thought my heart would come out of my mouth, when in desperation I took a long shot at his head; he continued, without slackening his pace; but in a second, the tracker seized hold of me as I was leaning against a tree quite beat, and made signs that he was down. I struggled on again, but only in time to see the huge brute regaining his legs, and scuttling off as fast as ever: I imagine the ball had stunned him for a second or so.

CHAPTER XX.

ALLIGATORS—TANK-WATER—COCOA-NUT-TREES—THE SEA.

26th.—ALL the elephants having disappeared, we also "concluded to travel;" we marched six or seven miles through the same picturesque, park-like country, as well stocked as ever with pig and pea-fowl, and encamped for breakfast near a small tank full of alligators, but we could not bag any.

Though apparently the most apathetic of reptiles, they are in reality very "wide awake." This peculiarity of wakefulness is more remarkable in them, inasmuch as they are gifted with three eyelids, instead of two, as is the case with most other animals. The snake has none at all. The alligators lay head to wind, and, whether owing to acuteness of scent or vision, they are certainly very hard to approach. There is another peculiarity, which gives the alligator anything but a prepossessing expression, namely, the total absence of lips, and the consequent display of enormous dagger-like teeth. Too liberal a display of pointed teeth is not always agreeable in the human species, giving the owner rather a hungry, vampire appearance ;—but then you feel that they only *look* unpleasantly sharp, whereas those of the alligator *are* so in reality. Foreigners always say that the English have long alligator-like teeth, and they account for it by our so continually cleaning them, and pushing up the gums; they certainly cannot often be accused of a like unprofitable expenditure of labour.

The tank-water, though partaking of all the hues of the rainbow, and varying in consistency from thin porridge to the usual limpid state, is generally healthy enough. It is certainly very disgusting, when almost parched with thirst, to come upon an ample supply of water of a green, or brown, or pink colour, and of any imaginable consistency but that of *aqua pura.*

However, there is matter for consolation in all the little ills and inconveniences of this life, if we will but suffer ourselves to examine them with an unprejudiced eye. If, for example, the tank-water, instead of being muddy, filthy, and undrinkable, were clear, sparkling, limestone water, we should more than once, when utterly parched with several hours' unceasing tracking, have drunk such quantities as would have materially shortened our days, by "bursting us right off," as a Yankee would say, or by a slower, though scarcely more enjoyable, attack of dropsy.

The tanks are covered with a sort of green weed, something resembling duckweed; and this, at the same time that it imparts a greenish hue to the water, and renders it unpalatable to the taste, possesses a remarkable power of filtering it, and rendering it perfectly innocuous, by attracting to itself all the animalculæ, which would otherwise be larking about in the fluid, and be probably swallowed by the thirsty soul, to his great harm and damage. The coolies are perfectly aware of this provision of nature, and drink with great caution of any tank-water where this weed or plant does not exist.

Some of the party shot some pea-fowl, which the coolies immediately seized (the legs at least) for "doctor's stuff;" they extract some oil from them, which they say is good for fractures or wounds. Several of the natives were suffering cruelly from dysentery, and were very anxious we should kill a monkey for them, as they affirmed that it contained some specific for the complaint: however, we did not see clearly how they were to be benefited; and shooting a monkey is so distressing a business, and so like shooting a man, that no one having once done so would willingly undertake it again.

28*th.*—Off at five, through chapped, sun-burnt paddy fields, in which were pea-fowl, hog, and jackals, without number. Punchy's disposition for mischief came out very strongly this morning. He had been very tiresome, attacking every cooly and horse in turn; when, losing my temper, I gave him a very tolerable thrashing, and dismounting, handed him over to his only friend, the horse-keeper. We had marched some two miles through deep sand, when we reached the side of a shallow river; not wishing to wet my feet, and then walk on again in the sand, I got on my friend's back to cross the ford. I suppose he perceived this was the moment for his revenge, for he allowed me to mount without any backing or rearing, a most uncommon occurrence, and walked quietly in the water till he reached the deepest part, when, without the slightest warning, down he went on his knees, thus wetting me much more than if I had walked through. When he had given me the dip, he seemed perfectly contented, and got up again without the least attempt to lay down. If animals could reason, I should have sworn this proceeding on the part of the pony was malice prepense, and it appeared as much the effect of premeditation, as any act I have seen performed by a human being.

We passed some tanks and lagoons, whose

banks were actually lined with water-fowl, ibis, teal, crane, &c. There are more alligators in this part of Ceylon than in any other, and the cocoa-nut estates in the neighbourhood lose on an average three coolies a-year from these carnivorous saurians; but notwithstanding their strength and daring, there appears little doubt that the natives could considerably lessen their number, if not eventually destroy them. They never fail when any "human," man, woman, or child, is taken by one of these monsters to catch him, which shows that they have the power of entrapping them when so inclined.

The more one learns of nature, the more exceeding wondrous appear her laws and dispositions. The alligator, which enjoys unusual immunity from the destructive propensities of man, both on account of its natural defences, and its entire uselessness when dead, might increase to such an extent, that the country would be overrun with them, had not nature, all provident, implanted in the animal itself the safety valve of its dangerous qualities, and by impelling it to become the destroyer of its own species, thus prevent its too dangerous increase. The male alligator destroys all the eggs that it can lay paw upon, and the female has to bury her embryo progeny, to protect them from the unnatural appetite of their Saturn-like papa. How wonderful are the resources of nature, and how different the instincts of her creatures in different lands! Whilst this is the conduct of the alligator, the ostrich, whose enemies are numerous, also breaks some of her eggs, but for a far different reason, viz. that in a parched and barren land, where food is scarce and laborious to procure, her youthful progeny may have something to support nature, directly they issue into the world. The caterpillar, more provident, deposits a sandwich or sausage. There are other creatures, however, besides, that destroy the youthful brood of alligators; a kind of tortoise, called the trionyx, and several kinds of monkeys are excessively partial to alligator's eggs and omelettes.

We breakfasted at a village called Agapato; it is inhabited, and the surrounding country owned, by the Moormen I have before mentioned. The bold inquisitive manner of these men, visible even in the little brats that could scarcely crawl, formed a very striking contrast to the cringing, timid manner of the Tamuls and Cingalese. A good deal, doubtless, is the effect of hereditary good living, but still more is to be attributed to the inherent energetic superiority of the race of Mussulmans over the inhabitants of India. They became so annoying during breakfast, and pressed so closely round us, that at length, finding all requests, whether mild or imperative, for more room, unavailing, we at last threatened to rub them all round with pork, a determination that soon scattered them to their village. The touch of pork, dead or alive, does not render a Mahommedan perfectly unclean, like the touch of a dead body, and a few invocations, a good washing of himself and his garments, soon again fit him for the society of his fellow Moslems, but still they have a great dread of it. I fancy they fear the contact with the unclean beast, more on account of the chaffing of their companions, than from any idea of its own intrinsic evil.

During breakfast they came to tell us a man had fallen from a cocoa-nut-tree, and asked us for physic, but unfortunately, though amply provided for cholera, fever, dysentery, and other jungle ailments, we had none for wounds or contusions.

It is curious to watch the celerity with which the natives, young and old, ascend the cocoa-nut-trees; they tie their feet together with a piece of cord, about a foot and a half long, and with that climb the tree by a succession of jumps, almost like a leech.

The districts of Batticaloe and Agapato, on the east coast, produce the finest cocoa-nuts in the island of Ceylon, and nearly all the best plantations, European or native, are in that neighbourhood. I could not with any certainty ascertain the exact cost of clearing and planting an acre of cocoa-nuts, or of the actual amount of profit, but one thing is very certain, viz. that the returns are far better on paper than in reality. Cocoa-nut estates are like atmospheric railways, electric clocks, and numerous other discoveries and inventions, perfect in theory and on paper, but for some reason or another, not set forth or ascertained, imperfect in practice. The predictions of the golden harvests to be yielded by the coffee estates were far exceeded by those to be gathered from the cocoa-nut plantations, and fortunes and monies were invested and wasted with equal celerity, and under equally sanguine anticipations of rapid and enormous profits. I think, however, cocoa-nuts are likely to be a far more remunerative property than coffee. When once planted and arrived at maturity, the cost of cultivation and cropping is excessively small. They require great care and attention and constant irrigation as seedlings, but they amply repay the care when arrived at their full growth. "Water me continually in my youth, and I will quench thy thirst abundantly during the rest of thy life," is an Hindoo proverb about the cocoa-nut, and, unlike some of its kindred, is actually true. The cocoa-nut is from seven to twelve years before it arrives at maturity, and it is that lengthened period of suspense, when year after year has to be passed without any more interesting occupation than constant watching, that renders its cultivation so much more suited to the tastes and habits of the native than to those of the European. The only exciting influences connected with cocoa-nut cultivation, are the chance of an extraordinary drought, which, even in the tenth or eleventh year, may destroy all the fruits of your labour and hopes of remuneration, and the attacks of a certain beetle, which furtively inserting its head into the thick part of the inside of the leaf, burrows its way into the heart of the tree itself; when frequently the first intimation the proprietor has of its presence, is the sudden and hopeless withering of the tree attacked. Beetle hunting is rather an exciting sport, and so it ought to be, considering its important results, and that it is the only sport or excitement the resident proprietor has to occupy him during the ten or twelve years. It is carried on with a strong barbed needle, which is jobbed into the leaf for the purpose of transfixing the destructive scarabæus, whose fate when in the hand of the enraged and perspiring proprietor, it is easy to imagine. One tree will produce from fifty to sixty nuts a-year, and these at a clear profit of a halfpenny per nut, will clear about one rupee, or two shillings. The trees bear all the year round, and the ripe fruit and the buds are visible on the tree at the same time.

After a short march of some five or six miles, along the side of a brackish lagoon, we crossed a small belt of trees, and came suddenly upon the sea. Although it was not many weeks since I had seen it, and had then parted with it without any regret whatever, I really now hailed it again, after the seemingly interminable and monotonous jungles, as an old friend. This seemed to be a feeling shared in common by all, for the coolies threw down their loads and all rushed into the waves like so many school-boys; or, to use a school-boy's more classical simile, like "the Ten thousand" after their travels. One of our party had not seen the sea for seven years, almost incredible when one remembers that Ceylon is an island, and moreover not a very large one.

It always appears to me that there is something very peculiar in the sensations and train of thought one experiences on the sea-shore, totally different from what one feels elsewhere. The present, whether prosperous or unhappy, seems entirely sunk; and our thoughts are carried, as it were, by "convection," across the dark, glancing, scintillating mass before us, freighted either with regrets or congratulations for the past, or with longings and uncertainty for the future. I fancy few men can sit alone on the sea-shore and cogitate on the present; their thoughts will imperceptibly glide into the past or into the future. Water is a bad conveyer of heat, but a good one of thought.

Columbus longing to seek new shores, and Robinson Crusoe pining to revisit old ones, would, on the sea-shore, find a panacea for present dangers and persecutions in visions of happiness past or to come. The first view of the sea after any absence, always leads one's thoughts back to the early days ("innocent!" they are called) of childhood, when the sea was seen for the first time, and digging sand with a crooked spade, and wetting one's feet in the advancing wave, were considered the greatest enjoyments life was capable of imparting. How few men there are who do not regret innumerable events since those days of childhood, but how much fewer is the number of those who would return to that childhood again!

"I would give the hopes of years for those bygone hours,"

is excessively pretty poetry, especially when set to music, but in reality it is untrue.

However old a man may be, there is always something he is striving for, and looking forward to, and which he expects will afford him more gratification than anything that has gone before and the chance of which he would not exchange for all the happiest hours of his past life, or retrace his life one single day, but for the purpose of ensuring with greater certainty his plans for the attainment of the desired object. It is very lucky it is so. Man, whether for good or for evil, is a progressive animal, and if continually regretting the past, and the happiness gone by, he would be at a stand-still. However, this is moralizing *sans cause* with a vengeance.

The coolies rushed first into the sea; and we had with difficulty brought them away from that, warning them of the multitude of sharks, when they rushed back across the narrow isthmus to the fresh-water lagoon, where the danger was equally great from alligators. We camped in a sacred grove of cocoa-nuts washed by the sea, and surrounding a Hindoo temple and car of Juggernauth—now apparently in the coachmaker's hands. The sea breezes were so delicious during the day, that we determined to halt for a couple of days to enjoy them; but woe to those, who trusting in the health-bearing breeze of the day, neglected any of the usual precautions against fever during the night.

About 10 P.M. the sea-breeze ceased, and the land-wind rolling lazily over miles of fœtid unwholesome marshes, blew from the contrary direction. Although the land wind is not nearly so cold as the sea-breeze, I awoke with a fit of shivering, and in a second perceived the atmospheric change that had taken place. More of our coolies took fever at that place than at any other where we camped.

The next day we had athletic games for half rupees amongst the coolies, races and jumping. We could not distinguish them by name, so were obliged to have recourse to those distinctive appellations they had earned during the present trip; most of them were distinguished by their diseases and ailings, such as "Sore Legs," Nos. 1, 2, 3; "Fever," up to the number of 10; "Sore Heels," Nos. 1, 2, 3; "Dysentery," up to the same number. Others were known by more high-sounding sobriquets; one handsome young boy was distinguished as the "Apollo Belvidere;" another as the "Sphinx," from a decided resemblance to that mutilated remains of Egyptian idolatry or oppression. The games were tolerably well contested, and they ran a deal further in the hot sun, through deep sand, for the sum of one shilling sterling, than I would have done. The foot races were won by the "Apollo," and the jumping by "Sore Heels," No. 1.

Moralizing by the "sad sea wave," I thought at first the inhabitants of this small community, with no cares, and scarcely any necessary employments, all their wants being supplied by prodigal Nature, without even the slightest exertion on their part, must be very happy; they ought apparently to have been Utopians; however, I was soon undeceived, for at dinner there came crowding round us a group of halt and sick, the most miserable, squalid, diseased objects, I have ever seen; one complaining of worms right up to his throat; others of hereditary sores, eating away their lives slowly, but surely, without any hope of remedy. I soon changed my belief, and satisfied myself that whatever diseases may be entailed by civilization, they are not greater than those which oppress man in his natural state, and that bad as civilized humanity may be, it yet affords a chance of relief, which wild nature does not.

Then again, the bestial degrading nature of the Hindoo and Buddhist faith, offering to its votaries no object of engrossing thought, either of duties for the present, or hopes or dread for the future, renders life to them a blank: they have not even the excitement of the chase, or of war, or the uncertainty of agriculture, to harden and string up their natures, and stimulate their energies. The worm that creeps slowly through life, its only object being to consume its food, and to escape being crushed, is almost as noble a creature as the emaciated, indolent, torpid Cingalese; his companions, the elephant and the hog, are far beyond him. These wretches were the most degraded and most miserable of the human race I had yet seen; even offers of money, that omnipotent unanswerable argument, failed to induce them to exert their unstrung sinews, they would not be persuaded by any offer of reward to cut grass for our horses, or climb a tree to throw down cocoa-nuts. It is curious, that, fifteen miles from this indolent set, should be located the energetic, hard-working, healthy race of Moormen; the contrast between them is to be traced to the difference of breed, and to the degrading effect of Buddhism, the most contemptible form of worship the world has ever seen.

CHAPTER XXI.

PICTURESQUE CAMP—COOLIE—DEATH IN THE EAST—KILLING BOARS—TENACITY OF LIFE—BEARS.

We left our camp early in the morning, and pitched our tent in a very picturesque spot, on the edge of a kind of lagoon, full of alligators; but though we tried hard, we were equally unsuccessful as in our former attempts at catching any.

The coolies lighted fires for the joint purpose of driving away the ants and mosquitos, and of frightening the elephants. The effect of these numerous fires lighting up the old forest trees, and the gigantic bush-ropes, or rather, cables, that stretched from one to the other, was very striking. The jungle was so dense that we had been forced to hang our tent in an elephant path, and when we turned in for the night, it was with the pleasant feeling, that we had every chance of being unceremoniously aroused, if any elephant, who had indulged too freely in the evening, should be seized with hot coppers during the night, and come down for a drink.

During our march the next morning, we passed what we thought was a dead coolie. The sight is so ordinary a one in Ceylon, especially on the roads which the coolies frequent in their migration to and from the mainland of India, that it scarcely attracts attention, unless one's horse shies at it, and then one follows the example of the Pharisee of old, of "passing by on the other side." We had all passed this body, when one of the party looking back at it, fancied he saw its white cloth move, and as there was no wind stirring, he immediately told us; so halting the coolies, we returned, and found on examining the object that it was a very old man, to all appearance perfectly dead; however, such was not the case, for on lifting him up we detected a slight quivering of the lips. We gave him some water, and in about ten minutes, his eyes opened, and he stared wildly about. We gave him a cocoa-nut, which he drank with starving eagerness, and then put him in charge of the horsekeepers, who, wrapping him in a horse-cloth, carried him to our camping-ground some mile and a half distant; here we fed him delicately on fruit, milk, and whatever we could to nourish him, and by degrees restored his strength so far as to enable him to tell his story He had been returning with a party of friends and relations from a pilgrimage to Kataragam, and falling sick, they kindly left him on the road, without anything to eat or drink, or any protection from the sun, till he should get stronger. We found him lying at the edge of a salt lagoon, and for three days and nights he had not tasted food or water; he had crawled to the lagoon, believing it to be fresh water, and one can imagine his agony and despair on finding it was salt, and that he had not strength to move away in search of more. When we discovered him, the pangs of death were over, and a very few minutes longer probably would have closed his existence. I doubt whether we conferred any benefit upon him by revivifying him, for supposing he ever recovered sufficiently to return to his friends, one cannot imagine that, having once deserted and left him for dead, his reappearance in the family circle would be a matter of much congratulation.

The more one sees of the world, the more one becomes convinced that one's existence and welfare is of far more importance to oneself than to any other person, and the feeling of selfishness thereby engendered does not improve our nature. We are often shocked to find how soon we are reconciled to the loss, or to the misfortunes, of our friends; and we cannot expect that they will bewail our individual sufferings to any greater extent. In India, where deaths are so sudden, you sup with a man one night, attend his funeral the next morning, and probably dine with some of his most intimate friends that evening, after attending the sale of his effects, this feeling of selfishness increases more than in Europe. A friend of mine in India told me that his death from cholera had been reported and credited, and the evening of the day on which the report reached the Presidency, he walked into the billiard-room of the club, and he said that his eyes were never more completely opened to the actual value and duration of friendship, and of the utter unimportance of any individual life to the general routine and amusement of society, than by finding his most intimate and affectionate friends playing and smoking, and chaffing away as usual, having, in a very few hours, got over the shock, and reconciled themselves completely to his sudden loss. Of course they were very happy to see him, and shook him by the hand, with "By Jove, old fellow, I thought you were dead," &c. &c. But an occurrence of that nature could not fail to prove to a man of the most moderate discrimination, that his existence was of remarkably little consequence, even in his own small world.

The difference between sickness and death in the East and in Europe is this: in India, as I have said, the last details are hurried over as quickly as possible; the blow is so sudden, the shaft from the quiver of the "rider on the white horse" dealt with so unerring an aim, that the shock is past almost before one is aware the blow has been struck; and when you see the man standing at your elbow struck down, your first feeling is one of selfish congratulation at having escaped a similar fate. In England it is different: there you see your friends sinking gradually, but surely, to their end; you may meet one apparently in the full enjoyment of health, but you know that the hand of death has set his seal, and that he will as assuredly claim that fair form within a certain number of weeks or months, as that night will succeed the day. The former may be compared to a gust of wind suddenly extinguishing the lamp that is in your hand; the latter, to a lamp which can last but a certain time, its light and brilliancy sink lower and lower, and become more feeble with every breath, and you watch the uncertain return of its flickerings with the painful, oppressive conviction that each one may be the last. I cannot help fancying that the former bereavement is the more bearable; and that what one is in the habit of attributing to a certain recklessness regarding death in India, is in reality nothing more nor less than habit.

We camped alongside a most feverish-looking tank, where, apparently, the Queen of Mosquitos held her court. Our water for the last few days had been very indifferent, displaying the prismatic hues to a degree that was not tempting: it varied in colour from green to blue, black to grey; the consistency also was subject to constant and exciting variety, from thick gruel to the thinnest milk and water, and this evening the fluid, if it deserved the name at all, was of a very decided orange colour, and about as thick as thin mustard. We were very thirsty, but it literally was undrinkable, and as the spoons and salt had not arrived, we could not make it palatable as "natural porridge." However, we were soon to witness one of those providential resources that nature has so liberally supplied to her children, if they will learn how to avail themselves of her bounty. We had got a quantity of the nauseous-looking fluid in a large chatty or pot, and after several unsuccessful attempts at a drink, were contemplating it with feelings of mingled despair and disgust, when one of the coolies, seeing our state of mind, went to a tree hard by, and immediately returned with some small berries, rather like overgrown hips and haws, or small dried cherries; with these he began rubbing the inside of the chatty—the effect was magical: in a second or so, the mud and dirt held in suspension began to curdle, as it were, and condense, leaving the surface and sides clearer; this effect continued till the whole curdled mass sank gradually to the bottom, leaving the water perfectly clear and palatable. The tree is somewhat like a cherry-tree; the nut is termed the Strychnos Potatorum, and is, I should imagine, the only individual of that particular family of plants that is not poisonous; its use is known and appreciated by all travellers in Ceylon. I am not aware of its existence in any other country; but certainly there can be none where its purifying qualities are more acceptable.

Towards sunset several deer and hog came down to bathe and take their evening drink; we allowed them to enjoy themselves unmolested for a certain length of time, hoping that perhaps the tank might be the "house of call" of some elephant, but as none made his appearance, we commenced an onslaught on the grovelling swine.

One of the pigs approaching to within five hundred yards of our camp, we fired several shots, long range, at him, of course not hitting him, though the balls fell pretty near. He apparently treated them with supreme contempt, and continued digging and ploughing with the utmost nonchalance; supposing from this that he might remain for a closer attack, two of my companions started round the tank for that purpose, narrowly escaping an enormous cobra that lay coiled up in their path, and which they only perceived at the moment it was preparing to strike. One outran the other, and when within thirty yards of the ancient hog, the animal perceived him. The hog is at all times a determined savage creature, and especially when enraged;

> "When bristled boars from beaten thickets spring,
> In grinded tusks, a thunderbolt they bring;"

and I fancy that though the old gentleman had not shown much discomposure at the numerous balls that had whistled round him, he had yet been cogitating over them, and saw in his aggressor their probable cause. Be that as it may, however, the boar charged at speed. D——, who had shot as many elephants as any man in Ceylon, was not to be daunted by a pig of any size or kind, and delivered both barrels with unerring precision; but the hog was not to be denied either, and continued his onset unchecked for a second, consequently there was no help for it, but away ran the sportsman in the direction of his companion, followed by his foaming enemy at best pace. As Aphrodite affectionately observed to her lover, when warning him against the tusked boar,

> "They know not how to spare a blooming age,"

and D——'s blooming age would certainly have been shortened by the enraged pachyderm, had not C—— at that moment broken into the animal's amusement with a couple of ounce balls in its vitals: even then he would not die till he had received four more leaden pills. His tenacity of life was certainly most remarkable; and as we were in a land where the philosophy of Pythagoras obtains, I could not help fancying that the carcase of the boar had been animated by the soul of St. Gengulphus, or "the living jingo," as he is more familiarly termed, and who was thus in another shape displaying that peculiar tenacity of life that, witnessed in the human shape, ensured his sanctity, and handed his reputation down to our days.

This tenacity of life in the pig is very remarkable, and renders him a most dangerous antagonist, as much so even as the elephant. It appeared that one of D——'s first two shots had entered the eye, and lodged in the head, and that the other had entered behind one shoulder and come out before the other. The hog when charging does so with a succession of springs, and with the speed of lightning, (it is almost as quick as the spring of a tiger,) using his razor-like tusks with a strength and rapidity that renders any chance of defence at close quarters almost hopeless. When angry he will attack anything; and more than one instance is on record where he has even turned upon and attacked an elephant when beating the jungle.

29*th*.—Short march of some four or five miles. The horse-keepers carried our old patient in a horse-cloth. We had fed and nourished him with milk and fruit, but he was too weak to pick up strength fast, and his thoughts wandered, but where, I could not understand.

When the camp was pitched we sent out our trackers to seek for elephant signs. This was expected to prove a sure find; deer, peacock, and hog were moving about in numbers, but, as usual, we left them unmolested. Just at sunset, however, a coolie, breathless with haste, and fiery hot with speed, arrived, saying there was a bear close to camp. Of course we were off in a second; we surrounded the thicket in which he was said to be, and pierced it in all directions, but although we could hear him grunt, and the coolies declared they saw him, *we* could not; it was annoying, being the only chance of a bear we had. The bears in Ceylon are very ferocious, and the three worst wounds I have seen inflicted by wild animals were by them; two in Ceylon, the one being the sick man we were nursing, and the whole of whose scalp and face had been torn off, and the other a young Englishman, a coffee planter; the third was an officer in India, whose face had been fearfully scarred by a "bar." The Cingalese have an especial horror of them, and in many jungles we traversed, refused to proceed unless in companies of two or three together. The ferocity of the female bear with cub, has always been proverbial, and I fancy the male shares the ferocious nature of its better half.

Most of our men by this time had had attacks of fever; some were recovering, but others were still very bad, so weak that they could scarcely walk, and to see them attempting their loads was very distressing. But there was no help for it: we had no beasts of burden but them, and if we had they could not have progressed through the intricate jungle tracks.

The elephants did not "show," but kept up an animated concert during the night, calling and answering each other. One could almost imagine that they were questioning one another about the strangers who had so unexpectedly appeared in their neighbourhood.

CHAPTER XXII.

HEADMAN—SUMMARY MEASURES—PICTURESQUE GROUP—EVILS OF TRAVEL—INSECTIVORA—EBONY—JUNGLE FEVER—ADJUTANT BIRD LOTUS—BETEL LEAF.

This morning the headman of the neighbouring village, whom we had sent for to take charge of the sick man, came into camp, accompanied by a long tail of admirers and dependents. He refused point blank to have anything to do with the business, and moreover displayed an amount of insolence that our dignity could scarcely allow to pass without notice. As we were several days' post from any court of appeal, and as the delay would probably have ended in the death of the poor old invalid, who got weaker and weaker every hour, we thought the emergency of the case warranted rather strong remedies, and therefore intimated to the combed and petticoated individual, who was chewing and expectorating in a most stercorateous manner, that, unless "ecdum" (a most expressive Hindostanee word for "right off," "immediately") he sent some men to carry the poor old fellow to the village, and supplied him with food and lodging when there, we should take the liberty of tying him, the headman, up to the nearest available tree, and of giving him such a taste of our stirrup-leathers as we doubted excessively would be to his liking. During this expression of our sentiments, we assumed the sternest possible aspect, and moreover accompanied the threats with very significant preparations, to show that we really were in earnest: the effect was instantaneous, and our friend, after gradually changing colour from the brightest of copper to the dirtiest of whitey-browns, and eating an immensity of dirt in the shape of apologies and salaams, consented to take immediate charge of our patient, undertaking to forward him, when sufficiently repaired, to his friends, wherever they might reside. For this service we consented to make him a handsome present of the sum of twenty shillings. The old patient was immediately taken to the village; but the next day, on passing through, we saw him weaker, and evidently nearer his latter end. So I fancy, poor old fellow, he did not exact much further attention from his mercenary nurses than that of providing him with a thin covering of his mother earth to keep off the birds of the air,—for I doubt very much whether the beasts of the field, unless "hard set," would have wasted any time over his emaciated frame.

We were off to the jungle early in the morning, confident of "raising some tails," if not "realizing" a pair of tusks—elephants having been heard during the night. We tracked for some hours, and then squatted in the dry, sandy bed of a river, under the shade of some ebony-trees, whilst our trackers prosecuted their search. Picture to yourself a group of hunters reclining at ease during the fierce heat of a tropical mid-day sun, under the umbrageous limbs of *some wide-spreading* ebony or banyan-tree; their occupations in perfect unison with their state of repose. One thirsty soul is perhaps sucking tea with patient perseverance from the small neck of a beer-bottle; another, dispensing with knife and fork, is discussing with anatomical precision the carcase of a chicken (or eight-penny, as they are there called); a third, extended on his back in luxurious tranquillity, is puffing the post-matutinal cheroot, and, opening wide the "fauces" or "chops," is watching with considerable interest the circles of smoke as they escape from his mouth, and gradually diffuse themselves into thin air; a fourth, of a more imaginative turn of mind, and, moreover, possibly already replete with tea and chicken, is reclining even more luxuriously, and with half-closed eye, is dreaming of other lands, and wondering perhaps whether his Betsy Ann is still really true to him, or whether she has "taken up with" another; or, it *is possible* (though barely) that he himself, forgetful of his Betsy, is recurring with pleasure to the thoughts of that lovely creature in a bright blue bonnet that he assisted to a cab just before leaving London! These agreeable thoughts and occupations are only momentarily interrupted by the sharp cry of the deer close at hand, or the roar of the elephant some miles away, or, it may be, by the stealthy motions of some juvenile monkey, as it noiselessly approaches to peer at the strange intruders, and then springs away in an agony of fear, its loud chattering taken up and repeated in chorus by its invisible companions. Close within reach lie the deadly rifles, with the more useful smooth bores, and at a short distance the turbaned horse-keepers and tucked-up steeds doze side by side, forgetful at once of ants and elephants.

Hundreds of *Polychromatic* birds (songsters, would suit the sentence better, but unfortunately the birds in Ceylon don't sing) sport in the higher branches, and clouds of butterflies—"the cynthias of the hour," that, large as larks and as flaunting as dahlias—

> "Make the rose's blush of beauty pale,
> And dim the rich geranium's scarlet blaze,"

flit and hover about, and in their "frank lustinesse," as Spenser has it, gambol amongst the gorgeous tropical foliage, and chase each other from mead to flower in apparently endless pastime, though it is really a matter of killing and eating.

What picture can be more delicious and enticing, and who would not give up the stale enjoyments of a smoky city for an hour of such an existence? But before the enterprising and enraptured cockney *does* give up the comforts and sports of his native land, let him first consider the reverse of the picture, and then decide. In the first place, three, probably, out of the four individuals thus reclining, are suffering from fevers, dysenteries, agues, leeches, or land-lice! The refreshing tea is probably sucked from a beery bottle; the chicken, from too close contact with the heated body of some nigger, has become disagreeably lukewarm; the cheroot, having been sat upon several times during the ride, can be made to answer no other purpose than that of exhausting the temper and lights of the smoker; the tree is still umbrageous, but every shaking twig or leaf causes one to glance furtively upwards, to see that no snake or scorpion is crawling above you, ready to plump on your nose at any moment. You may, indeed, close your eyes—in fact, that you probably would do—to keep out the eye-flies that swarm around you, but as for sleeping, or ruminating on anything peaceful or agreeable, the red ants, almost as large as wasps, or the soothing hum of Brobdignagian hornets, of bat-like dimensions, entirely put that out of the question. It is my humble opinion that the annoyances, and heat, and dirt of an out-door existence in a tropical country far exceed any pleasure or benefit to be derived from it. I would rather shoot a grouse on a hill-side in Scotland, or follow the fox across any *tolerable* country in England, than return a second Gordon Cumming, in the matter of wild sports. Then oh, ambitious Briton, "crede experto," trust one who has tried, and stay at home.

Ceylon is, in truth, the paradise of insectivora. The worms attain the length of three or four feet, the beetles are the size of mice, the ants of wasps; spiders' webs are tough enough to pull one's hat off, and the bite of a hornet or a wasp is sufficient to swell you up like a human toad. All these animals, and many others, are most tender and unceasing in their attentions to strangers, and "pasture on the pleasures of each place," whether nose, eyes, mouth, or ears, with a zest and pertinacity that is anything but soothing to the owner of the soil.

After this long digression, I may continue the thread of the narrative, which, probably, the reader has by this time forgotten. We remained scratching, and dozing, and grumbling, till long after midday, when the trackers returned, with elongated countenances, and announced they could find "no sign." So we returned, disconsolate and discontented, to camp.

We were now, and had been for several days, in the land of ebony (I mean the vegetable, not the animal), and we passed numerous gangs of "lumberers" hewing and fashioning these valuable trees, preparatory to the rainy season, when they would be dragged to the rivers, and floated down to the coast, and thence towed by native budgerows or Patamars up the coast to Colombo. The cutters were all Moormen, and, although in the centre of their country, there was not one Cingalese amongst them. They were cutting by contract for the Colombo merchants, and undertook to deliver logs twelve feet long by one foot square on the coast for ten shillings, paying, moreover, the sum of eightpence for every tree cut down, to the government. The value and beauty of ebony does not require much remark: it is to my mind the most handsome, as it is the most solid and enduring material for drawing-room furniture. Its great weight and hardness, however, render it too expensive for very general use even in Ceylon, the most fruitful land of its growth, and where it can be procured in any quantities, at the price I have mentioned.

It struck me that the number of trees destroyed by the Moormen in search of suitable ones for their market far exceeded those actually fashioned and floated down to the coast. However, the ebony forests are government property, which will to a very considerable extent account for the waste visible in their management. The satin-wood-tree also flourishes in great quantities, but its abundance in more available districts prevents those on the east coast from being much interfered with just at present.

31*st.*—Off early in the morning with a mendacious Moorman, whom may Sathanas, the father of lies, reward according to his deserts! Hoping to get the reward we daily offered for the discovery of a herd of elephants, he seduced us from our mosquito curtains, at some very small hour in the morning, with a circumstantial lie about a herd and a tusker, and conducted us through the most impenetrable of jungles and most fœtid of marshes, till near midday; when, as he had shown us no sign of elephant, but only the old footprints of alligators and buffaloes, we declined following any longer, and returned to camp in no very amiable mood, and I fear were not particularly complimentary in our language to the Moorman, who had been the cause of our fruitless and feverish hunt. Such an agueish, unhealthy morning's work I never remember to have undergone; in many places the stench was actually so great as to be almost stifling. I felt convinced some of the party must catch fever, and I was not mistaken, for that very day our Cingalese servant, who up to that time had been perfectly hearty, and eager for the fray, *carrying* guns all day, and *cleaning them* all night, complained of fever, and in a couple of hours was so weak and prostrate as to be unable to walk without support; so wonderfully rapid is the progress of jungle fever! A young Cingalese tracker also, the most active of the party, was the next day utterly unfit for work, and was obliged to return to his village and friends. The fever is most active in its onslaught, and generally attains its culminating point of intensity at midday and midnight. Quinine is the only remedy that at all mitigates its violence, and the doses we administered to our patients, often without any visible effect, would, I imagine, have astonished the College of Physicians.

The swamps through which we passed were actually teeming with wild birds of all imaginable shapes and sizes, chiefly waders, to say nothing of scores of alligators. The most striking of the waders, both in size and appearance, is the adjutant bird. It is one of the largest of birds, measuring from five to seven feet in height, and fifteen feet from tip to tip of its ponderous wings. They stand in long lines at the edges of the swamps, perfectly motionless, intently regarding the water, and watching for some silly little fish to come within reach. When thus occupied, and seen from a distance, they present a most ludicrous appearance, bearing an exact resemblance to a number of bald-headed niggers fishing. They do not, however, confine themselves to the sport of fishing, but are remarkably omnivorous in their disposition, turtles ten inches long and full-grown cats having been discovered in their "mofussils," or interiors, when shot; they moreover attack and destroy the largest kind of snakes. In India they are esteemed sacred, and are supposed to be animated by the souls of deceased Brahmins. They are sometimes very annoying, and even dangerous, and that in rather a remarkable manner: they frequent in numbers the neighbourhood of barracks, or any other place where they can find the means of making themselves comfortable on plenty of garbage, and being very torpid and lazy, they will not get out of the way of those passing, but prefer pecking at them if they disturb their ease. As they feed entirely on offal and other refuse, their beak is generally tainted and poisoned with decayed animal matter, and if they manage to break the skin, the wound is often of the most dangerous nature. The same latent poison exists in the claws of tigers, panthers, cats, hawks, and in fact, any carnivorous animal. The fact, perhaps not generally known, of the scratch of the old cat being more venomous than that of the kitten, arises from the claws of the former having become hollowed by age, and therefore containing far more poisonous matter.

More than three-fourths of our party had now had attacks of fever or some other ailment, and we consequently thought no time was to be lost in seeking for more healthy hunting grounds.

In the evening we shifted camp to the borders of another large tank. It must have occupied an area of several hundred acres, and was entirely covered with the pink lotus; a considerable portion of it was in blossom, and the brilliant pink of the splendid flowers contrasted agreeably with the sombre hue of the surrounding foliage. The lotus is almost as much connected with the traditions of the Buddhist and Hindu religions, as it was with the idolatry of Egypt in olden days. Many of their similes and proverbs are derived from, or connected with, their ideas of the lotus. It is the emblem of beauty, and a father addresses his son as my "lotus-faced boy," "my *cheeild* with the lotus chops," much as affectionate parents in England address their young hopefuls as "my handsome boy," "my lovely youth." The seed of the lotus flower, after the blossoms have fallen away, are remarkably good eating, and resemble filberts scarcely ripe. The coolies brought us large quantities of them, and with salt and a glass of sherry, we found it very easy to imagine ourselves discussing an autumnal dessert in England.

In the evening a large herd of wild buffalo visited the tank, and performed their evening ablutions; they were too far off for us to attempt to stalk them that evening; moreover, we were as usual fearful of disturbing the elephants. We also ourselves meditated more extensive ablutions than the muddy water of the last week had rendered agreeable, or even practicable; but unfortunately, or I should rather say fortunately, just as we were denuding ourselves for the preparatory dive into the tank, a Cingalese kindly volunteered the information that there were plenty . . . . (some unintelligible word, which, however, signifies alligators), so we were obliged, coolie-like, to stand on the fallen trunk of a tree, on the brink, and content ourselves with pouring chatties of water over our heads.

Flocks of toucans, (not like the South American bird so called,) herons, sacred kites, and other large birds, seemed to have made the piece of forest in which we had pitched our camp, their sleeping quarters. They arrived in flights just before sunset, but being afraid to roost in the immediate neighbourhood of such suspicious strangers, they took up their position on neighbouring trees, and commenced a chattering and croaking of a most discordant nature. Cingalese mythology inculcates the belief that birds and beasts had formerly the gift of speech; if they retain the faculty at present, I have no doubt our friends were in their own language conversing rather unkindly about us, for so unceremoniously invading their dormitories. They remained discoursing on the subject for some hours after their usual bed-time, when, with increased clamour, they betook themselves to some other location.

The mosquitos were very plentiful, and kept our followers in a most disagreeable state of liveliness all night. When camping with coolies, the annoyance of these "devil's trumpeters" is twofold, for not only do you suffer from the pressing attentions and cheerful hum of these lively little insects themselves, but your attempts at a doze are rendered, if possible, even more hopeless, by the monotonous, uninterrupted drone, with which the wretched coolies, totally unprotected from the bites, and half choked with the smudges round which they are huddled, try in vain to beguile the tedious night.

A village situated some three miles from our encampment, was celebrated for its abundance of betel-leaf, and we consequently had to keep a very sharp supervision over the masticating and expectorating propensities of our coolies. The betel is a creeper, somewhat like the vine, or rather, the vanilla creeper of South America, and has a fat succulent leaf, not very unlike the lilac, with a highly aromatic, and by no means disagreeable flavour. A little chunam, or prepared lime, and a piece of areca nut, are wrapped up with this leaf, and with the addition of a few cloves, cardamums, and cinnamon, the quid is far from unpalateable. All the requisites for betel chewing are found in great abundance in Ceylon and consequently throughout the island, from the child of three years to the old crone of eighty, men and women chew and expectorate with a perseverance that excites one's surprise at the strength of their jaws, and the abundance of their saliva. The juice of the betel-leaf combining with the chunam and areca nut, renders the saliva a deep blood red, and when a party of natives have been squatting for any length of time in one spot, you might almost fancy they had all been suffering from severe bleeding at the nose. The extent to which the habit of chewing betel existed in bygone years, may be gathered from the fact, that in the city of Kanouje, a former capital of Hindostan, which was destroyed by the firebrand, Mahmoud of Ghuznee, somewhere about the time of our Norman William, there were 30,000 vendors of betel. Whether betel, as is asserted by the learned, is the Malabathrum mentioned by Horace,* I cannot take upon myself to determine; but I should think it improbable.

* Horace, Ode ii. 7. Pliny, xii. 26.

CHAPTER XXIII.

THE HEADMAN—BRIBERY AND CORRUPTION—THE TANK—ELEPHANTS—EXCITING BREAKFAST.

Sept. 2.—OFF very early into the jungle; but though we toiled all day, we found nothing. We were getting slightly disgusted; for although we heard the elephants every night trumpeting and roaring in numbers, all our endeavours to cultivate a closer acquaintance during the day were unavailing. The ground was, as I have said, rather harder than any ordinary burnt brick; and, except in the sandy beds of rivers, and at the edges of tanks, we had no chance whatever of tracking with success. As I before remarked, I am not so excruciatingly fond of shooting; and I confess that more than once, if I could have laid my hands on a *Times* newspaper, and what Milton calls a "pure ambrosial weed," in other words, a real Havannah cigar, I should have been tempted to remain in camp, rather than labour in vain through a blistering sun after the half-reasoning game, that to my mind displayed far more sense in trying to avoid our society, than we did in seeking theirs. I think I should have been tempted to remain in camp, even without the cigar and the *Times*, had I not had the annoying conviction, that if I did remain at home, the others were sure to have sport.

More coolies falling sick, we determined to remove our camp to a large tank called Kitlani. It was the last cover in our route, and Duff, our honoured "Dux," had never once known it drawn blank.

As we were preparing to leave the camp, the headman of the village, who had refused to receive our old patient some days before, appeared with rather a sheepish look, attended by some half dozen natives bearing milk and fruit. He came straight up to me, and making a salaam, presented these gifts. Being rather surprised at this delicate attention from a man to whom I had certainly not addressed the most courteous language imaginable, I inquired the reason, when I found it was a peace-offering made by our friend to turn away our wrath, and to accompany a request that we would not report him to the government agent, as we had threatened to do. As I had, perhaps, been the most indignant and energetic in my threats on our former meeting, I suppose he imagined that my wrath would be the most enduring. He had discovered my weakness for milk from the old Apoo; and, with very tolerable philosophy, sought to gain my heart by gratifying my palate. We received him with an unrelenting air; impressed upon him the enormity of his offence, and the certainty of his being removed by the government agent, if not of his being hung; when we had sufficiently worked upon his terrors, we very gradually relented, and, with a magnanimity of the most gracious kind, tendered him our forgiveness, on condition he never did so again; and then, *proh pudor!* we "set to," on the milk and fruit. According to strict morality, there can be little doubt that we were quite wrong in receiving these gifts. It is but too probable that the offering of the headman was not actually his own to give, but that he had forced the poor villagers to supply the amount of the bribe; and that, like king Jehoiakim, when he gave gold and silver to Pharaoh-nechoh, he had "taxed the land to give the money;" now although we were hardly guilty of receiving a bribe to induce us to neglect a duty, inasmuch as we never had any intention whatever of performing it; yet we certainly sinned in "assuming a virtue when we had it not," and in taking a reward for omitting what we never intended to execute. The headman told us the old man was still alive and better, but I doubted excessively at the time whether he had not already put him out of the way, and had made this visit quite as much for the purpose of ascertaining our movements as of securing our good offices.

We found Kitlani decidedly an improvement on our former camping ground. The jungle was less dank and confined and unhealthy, and the coolies appeared to pick up a little health and strength.

At 3 P.M., not having received any decided news from our trackers, we strolled about two miles to a large tank, and there sat down, in the hope some elephants might resort thither to quaff their evening draught of muddy water. The tank was about three quarters of a mile across, and about two miles in length, of an oval shape. It was covered with lotus, and was filled rather with soft oozing mud and slime, than with water.

Sitting, Robinson Crusoe like, on a rock, and watching the motions of a water-buffalo wallowing, we debated as to the possibility of crossing the tank, and came to the conclusion that it was quite impossible even for the lightest of the party to advance any distance without being completely immersed. Numbers of deer, wild hog and buffalo came to the opposite side to drink. These animals, wandering about utterly unconscious of the presence of man, the declining sun lighting with its soft golden rays the dark interminable forest, and the calm tranquil aspect of the tank, rendered the scene one of quiet and attractive beauty.

"As a servant earnestly desireth the shadow," &c. so were we earnestly looking forward to the half-hour before sunset, when the elephants usually "liquor up;" we were thinking that "our shadows were very long in coming," or in other words, that the time passed slowly, when suddenly the head tracker, without moving a muscle, hissed out, "Arnee;" we followed the direction of his gaze, and sure enough just opposite to us we saw the jungle slowly open, and a huge mass issue forth, with that deliberate "swag," so peculiar to elephants. We remained perfectly still, and had the pleasure of seeing six full-grown ones, and one punchy, successively emerge, and follow each other with the same measured tread some thirty or forty yards into the tank. We were certainly more than half-a-mile from them, but with a small pocket telescope we examined them at our leisure, and arranged our order of battle accordingly; our plan was evidently to cut them off from the forest and drive them into the tank, where, as we supposed they could not pass, they must turn and fight. We accordingly doubled round the tank a distance, I should imagine, of rather more than a mile, keeping just within the edge of the jungle, till we were opposite our friends, when forming in *order of battle* we advanced out to meet them. Their first impulse was to retire further into the tank; but when they had got in some hundred yards or so, a fastidious old female, the leader of the party, turned half round, evidently with the determination of charging. Elephants do this in rather a remarkable manner; unlike most other animals, such as the hog, buffalo, &c., that fix their glance before they break into a charge, the elephant moves his body more than half round before he turns his head in the direction he intends to take. In this case the old lady charged with the evident intention of doing mischief; she received three or four balls in the head without flinching, but the fifth brought her low with a deep groan; the other six or seven elephants, I forget exactly the number, were now seized with a panic, and getting the little one in front of them, they hurried, huddled up like a flock of sheep, right into the tank; on the instant, forgetting alike all caution and former conclusions as to the impracticability of crossing, we dashed after them as fast as the mud would allow us. The race was most even, the broad feet of the elephant giving them if anything a slight advantage over their pursuers. In vain we strained nerve and heart to get ahead of them. We could reach their shoulders, but could not get one inch further. We fired in the hope of turning them, but without the slightest effect; their intense fear quite overcame any feeling of rage or agony that might have prompted them to show fight. After desperate exertions I had gradually crept up to the shoulder of one enormous brute; the muzzle of my gun was within two feet of him, and in hopes of making him turn, I fired both barrels behind the ear; but I might just as well have fired into a hayrick. Of course at the moment I was highly disappointed at the failure of my attempt; but in talking it over with my companions who witnessed the affair, I unwillingly came to the conclusion, that if he had attempted to charge, I was so close to him, that he must in the act of turning have inevitably extinguished my vital spark in the mud; so I am very glad he did not.

The tank had got deeper and softer, and we sank up to our waists—often up to our armpits, at every step. The pace of both pursuers and pursued had dwindled down to a laborious progression of about half a mile an hour. The elephants were gaining on us, when one of them, galled, I suppose, and enraged at repeated shots in the rear, faced about with the intention of charging, but immediately got a quietus in the shape of two or three bullets in the forehead. The others, however, still continued their course straight across; and we our exhausting pursuit. It was like toiling through snow four or five feet deep; now you trod on a crust that supported you, and the next step sank up to the shoulders. Our ammunition was all wet in our pockets, and we had to hold our guns well aloft to keep them fit for use. Being almost exhausted, and the elephants evidently keeping their own, we were on the point of relinquishing the chase, when frightened, I suppose, by the increasing softness of the ground, they suddenly made a sort of half turn in their course, which enabled us, by making one last dying struggle, to get up to close quarters again. We should, I think, have bagged two or three, but for the self-devotion of a male elephant who had hitherto protected the rear, but who now, finding us approaching, gallantly faced about, and flourishing his trunk, and trumpeting shrilly, attempted to charge; but, poor brute, he was too weak, and the ground too soft for him to move at any pace above the slowest trot; he could not, therefore, revenge himself with any very great effect. We gave him two or three shots in the forehead, when he sank on his haunches like a dog: it being next to impossible to touch an elephant's brain when in that position, we waited till he rose again, which he did in about a minute, his eyes actually starting from his head with concentrated rage and agony. We were now close to him, and his death was assured. Poor brute, it appeared a bloodthirsty proceeding, and I was very glad when his sufferings were ended.

We were up to our waists in mud, and were so helpless, in the case of a charge, that had he been strong, he might with ease have destroyed the whole party. Our only chance of escape, as we settled afterwards, would have been to have submerged ourselves entirely, and to have hid our diminished heads under some lotus leaf. This last charge, like that of Charlemagne's famous Paladin at Roncesvalles, although unavailing to himself, secured a retreat for his companions; and although we continued the chase to the opposite bank, any farther chance of overtaking them was hopeless. It was almost dark when we reached the bank; and, really, when I threw myself down on dry land, I don't know that I ever felt so completely exhausted—every muscle and every nerve had been at full stretch, under considerable excitement, for nearly an hour and a half. Our chance of being crushed by the elephants, or smothered in the mud, was agreeably varied by the prospect of being shot by some of the gun-carriers, who, in their excitement, (their nerves never being of the very best,) floundered about with guns at full-cock, or hammers on the nipples; and with muzzles pointing in every imaginable direction, from their masters' heads to their own stomachs, none of which circumstances conduced much to our chance of reaching the opposite side in safety. One unfortunate coolie, up to his shoulders in mud, in handing a gun to his master, also in the same hampered position, let off both barrels close to his own head; but so great was the excitement, that I, who happened to be rather nearer than the rest of the party, was the only one present, excepting his master, who was aware that any accidental discharge whatever had taken place. Another of the party, calling upon his gun-carrier for his second gun, had the pleasure of receiving one already discharged, and did not discover his error, till, advancing close to the elephant, he had the satisfaction of hearing both hammers click one after another, without so much as the explosion of a copper cap.

This evening's amusement was certainly the cream of elephant shooting, and I doubt, if a man were to follow that sport for fifty years, whether he would ever see the like again. Duff, who had himself shot somewhere about a hundred elephants, and had been present at the death of three times that number, confessed he had never seen anything like it. We missed him immediately after entering the tank, and he did not join us till the devoted charge of the last elephant. It appeared that just as he was coming out of the jungle with us into the tank, he saw another elephant in the jungle, and fearing lest he might take us in our rear, whilst engaged with the main body, he remained to watch, and if possible to shoot the animal; he failed, however, in the latter attempt. Veteran hunters will probably say we ought to have bagged more elephants, and that we bungled, &c. &c. &c. Very likely we did; but considering that, with the exception of D——, we were all "griffs;" and allowing for our position when shooting, I think we did very well; be that as it may, we were very well satisfied, and returned to camp in high spirits at this, the best day's sport we had yet seen. I was very much struck with the irresistible force and frightful velocity with which the last elephant flourished his trunk; and in talking over the subject afterwards, and discussing the extraordinary power possessed by the elephant in that member, D——, amongst other instances, mentioned having seen an elephant completely smash the back of a Water Buffalo, a very strong animal, with one blow of its trunk. I know of no object in nature, not even the human hand, which combines such delicate mechanism with such irresistible power as an elephant's trunk. One has been apt to consider Nasmyth's steam-hammer, which can with one blow exert a force of two tons, and with another, break a nut without injuring the kernel, as a triumph of human ingenuity, and so it is: but how insignificant, when placed in comparison with the trunk of an elephant; for not only can the latter strike a blow of a ton or so, and break an egg or a nut, but it can pick up a pin from the floor, or pull down a tree; project water with the force of a 20-man power forcing-pump, or uncork and drink a bottle of soda-water without spilling a drop!

Early next morning we were off to the forest, and after tracking without success for several hours, we sat down in the bed of a river, under a large silk-cotton-tree, and, as usual, proceeded to discuss our breakfast. We were in the midst of our meal, talking over the sport of the preceding day, when suddenly one of our horse-keepers hissed out the usual note of alarm, "Arnee," and on looking down stream, we saw an elephant leisurely descending the bank into the bed of the river, scarcely two hundred yards below us. He was closely followed by three others, the rear being brought up by a large elephant without any dorsal termination whatever, having been probably deprived of that precious appendage in some former encounter with the destructive white man. The four leading elephants swaggered across the river in most deliberate style, looking neither to the right hand nor to the left, and, ascending the opposite bank, entered the jungle: the tail-less party was lazily preparing to follow, when, as bad luck would have it, one of our horses neighed; the elephant immediately faced about at the strange sound, probably heard for the first time, and then made a hasty retreat after his companions. Every moment was now precious; so throwing down our half-emptied bottles of tea, and half-picked bones of chicken, we rushed after them, and dashed pell-mell into the jungle at the spot where they had disappeared; but our headlong course was soon arrested, for so dense and impenetrable was the underwood, that we could only advance one by one, and then with great difficulty. It was foolish in the extreme, to attempt an attack under such disadvantages; however, excitement had quite usurped the place of caution, so, following D——'s example, who had up to this time been preaching caution to me, and had frequently expostulated with me on the absurdity of rashness in particular, and of attacking elephants in bad jungle, in general, we made the best of our way after the trackers, who had hit on the trail of the elephants.

So close was the jungle, that we were bent half double; and Duff, who was leading, was actually on his knees, when he caught sight of the two hindermost elephants; he made a beautiful shot in that confined position, striking one on the forehead, "plum centre;" the huge beast fell up against his companion, and so hampered was the latter with the density of the jungle, and his wounded companion, that he could not clear himself sufficiently fast to charge his aggressors, as he evidently intended to do, till he had received two shots, which, though not fatal, had the desired effect of changing his mind, and causing him to sheer off in a contrary direction; we saw no more of him. The dead one was a large male. Had the elephant effected his charge, we must have come to great grief, as we were huddled up together in a narrow elephant path, in a crouching position, with such dense jungle on either hand, that getting out of the way of the charge, or even throwing ourselves down, was impossible. Whilst we were engaged in this manner, it appeared another elephant, who was following his companions, had trotted up the track in which we were; he had turned tail on seeing the trackers, but had he charged us in the rear, and his friend in the front, we should have been in a most unpleasant fix. All this took place about 600 yards from where we were breakfasting, and we returned to our half-eaten meal within a quarter-of-an-hour; rather an exciting interlude in a pic-nic breakfast, and one that would have created a slight sensation in some al fresco parties in England.

We remained under the same tree, in the same position all day, awaiting our trackers; about four o'clock they came in with intelligence of a "rogue." We rode some four miles down the river, and dismounting, entered the forest; we immediately came upon quite fresh sign, and very soon saw the elephant at some distance; he broke away at once, and we followed him at our best pace; it was very severe running; in fact, as hard as we could lay legs to the ground. After a smart burst, the elephant beat us fairly, and was very soon beyond pursuit; he was in a hideous fright, and fear seemed to have lent him wings, for he went almost as fast as a horse.

CHAPTER XXIV.

TAMARIND-TREES—PUNCHY—FEMALE ELEPHANTS—THUNDERSTORM—MAJOR ROGERS—TEMPLE—NEWERA ELIA.

NEXT day we started off early to a river about ten miles distant, said to have abundance of game in its neighbourhood. I started on foot, intending to ride later; but Punchy took it into his head to elude the vigilance of his horsekeeper, and enjoy a private lark of his own with some village cows; he was at last caught after considerable loss of time and difficulty, but too late for me to ride.

Our route lay through very close jungle, said to be so infested by bears, that the natives would not traverse it under parties of twos and threes. We worked hard all the morning, but without success, and at midday coming upon an encampment of Moormen, cutting ebony, we breakfasted. They were, as usual, excessively fine men, and their mental and physical superiority over their Cingalese compatriots were equally conspicuous. After the midday repast, they performed their usual ablutions and prostrations in the direction of the shrine of the prophet, and then returned to their work. Our Tamul coolies, and Cingalese guides, *never* prayed, for the very good reason that they never had anything whatever to worship. We continued tracking all day, chiefly in the beds of rivers. The sand was very soft and deep, and the footmarks of every animal or bird that crossed it were distinctly visible. We saw the trail in the sand of some very large snakes; some must have been nearly as thick as one's leg; the elephant spoor was really almost as thick, as I before remarked, as the footmarks of sheep on a dusty road; there must have been scores in the neighbourhood, and it was excessively aggravating not being able to "realize" any.

We had had a very hot day's work, and coming to some tamarind-trees, we halted, and filled our pockets with the fruit; it was scarcely ripe, but the acidity alleviated our thirst. The tamarind-tree is sacred to the chief of the devils, and like the Upas-tree, its exhalations during the night are said to be fatal,—both to man and beast, who may sleep under it, but that I believe is imaginary. It is supposed by Pundits, that the scriptural simile of the "wicked in great power, spreading himself like a green bay-tree," is an allusion to the tamarind-tree. The wood is excessively hard, and it never sheds its leaves. Punchy was so disagreeable in his increasing attempts to bite my feet, or his next neighbours, whether *bi* or *quadruped,* that I dismounted and handed him over to his only friend the horse-keeper; he followed him tolerably well for a mile or so, till we came to an open patna, where was a large herd of water buffalo feeding, when I suddenly heard a cry of distress, and turning round, saw Punchy dragging his unfortunate attendant, who had dropped his bundle, and lost his turban, at full speed across the rough ground, to the imminent danger of his neck, and the utter derangement of his person, neighing and kicking up his heels, followed by the whole herd of buffalo, wondering, and more than half terrified, at the exhibition.

An old Cingalese had joined our camp the day before, and accompanied us on our hunting trip; he was a headman, and evidently a man of the highest consideration amongst his countrymen; he was by way of being, a wit, and kept all the coolies and trackers in a roar of laughter; their respect and attention to him was, however, accounted for, by the fact of his being "*dives Malabathri et Pecudum,*" rich in betel and cattle.

The old saw, "*Chi ha quattrini ha amici,*" is as true in the wilds of Ceylon, as in the metropolis of Europe.

7th.—In the afternoon we went to the tank where our grand engagement had taken place some days previously. The elephants had swelled and burst, and herds of wild hog were now discussing their contents. They eat elephants with the greatest gusto, and as many as a dozen have been seen, when disturbed, scampering from the interior of one elephant. We had occupied our old position on the rock for several hours, and were getting rather impatient; when, about half an hour before sunset, we descried two old elephants and two punchies stalk deliberately out of the jungle at the extreme end of the tank, and proceed into the water. We immediately started off to intercept them; they were at least a mile distant, and the run across the dried margin of the tank, perforated with elephant spoor, holes some eighteen inches deep and about four feet in circumference, was very hard and dangerous work. The falls were numerous, and from the excessive hardness of the ground, most painful. Shakspeare, whose knowledge of natural history is not always the most correct, talks of "elephants being betrayed with holes, bears with glasses, unicorns with trees,"

&c. &c., but my experience would lead me to believe that the former betray with holes much more frequently than they themselves suffer in that way. D—— outran the party and came first to the elephants; he had seen them move, and cut off their retreat. The old one turned sharp round at his approach, but, as usual, a single shot laid her low. D—— continued his meteor course (to use a poetical simile), and overtaking the two young ones, dropped each of them with a single ball; thus bagging his three elephants with three shots; not bad work! As the female generally turns to protect her young, we now made sure of the fourth, an enormous female; but in this instance personal nervousness overpowered natural affection, and leaving her progeny to be deprived of life and shorn of its caudal termination by our ruthless coolies, she scuttled off into the jungle at a pace that defied all our attempts to overtake her. This want of feeling in a mother elephant is so rare, that I hardly believe the punchy could have been her own. I rather imagine it must have belonged to some lady friend, who had perhaps asked her "to take it out for a walk, and let the little dear pick some lotus in the Kitlani Tank." Elephants never have more than one at a birth, but females are frequently met with two or three young ones, of different sizes; so there is little doubt that lady elephants either hire themselves out as nursery governesses, or in a neighbourly way take charge of their friends' babas.

These were the last elephants we shot, and the next day we "lifted" camp en route to Badula. Altogether I had enjoyed the trip excessively; the sport is doubtless very exciting, though I own my pleasure was leavened with a considerable amount of compunction, at slaying a noble animal for no earthly object but my own amusement. The unhealthiness of the jungle is also a considerable drawback to the feeling of perfect enjoyment, for though individually we Europeans were entirely free from fever, yet the universal sufferings of the coolies could not but affect our pleasure most materially.

During the march in the early morning, the leading coolies ran back without their loads, and said an elephant was standing in the road. We hurried forward, but found none; a herd of hog, however, crossed at the moment, making far more noise than the same number of elephants would have done. The road was intersected at almost every half mile by "nullahs" some thirty feet deep and thirty or forty feet broad. The descent and ascent were very steep, and great equine steadiness was requisite to pass them in safety. Punchy's conduct was most aggravating; when about half-way down the descent, he invariably made a rush and a spring, in order to get an impetus up the other side. I did all I could to impress upon him the danger attending this course of proceeding, both to his knees and my neck; however he would take no warning, and at length in crossing one of the steepest, the event I had anticipated took place, for down he came with a tremendous crash, and over we rolled to the bottom; he cut his knees, and very nearly broke my ankle, disabling me completely as it was, and causing me acute suffering for some days.

We camped in a bungalow built for the government agent; late in the evening we had a most glorious thunderstorm. The lightning and thunder were contemporaneous, and the former beautifully vivid.

It is a curious electrical or meteorological fact, that nearly all the lightning in Ceylon is negative; which means, that the earth is positive, and the clouds negative—the lightning proceeding from the former to the latter. A remarkable instance of this peculiar arrangement of electrical agency happened at the lamented death of Major Rogers, the prince of elephant shots, the slayer of thousands, I believe. He had taken refuge with some ladies in a bungalow about half-way between Badula and Newera Elia, and went out into the verandah to ascertain if the storm had ceased; he had scarcely crossed the threshold, when he dropped down dead. On examination it was discovered that the electric fluid had entered at the heel, probably or possibly attracted by his spurs, and had caused instantaneous death. It was a singular death for a man who had for years exposed himself to the dangers of elephant shooting, and whose escapes and adventures are almost fabulous. On one occasion an elephant caught him with his trunk, and placing him between his fore and hind feet, tossed him from one to the other for a considerable space of time, breaking his thigh and several ribs during the amusement; Major Rogers preserved his presence of mind through this frightful situation of peril, and remained perfectly motionless, feigning death. The elephant, when satisfied with tossing him about, placed him in front, and prepared to kneel upon him; they happened to be on a slight incline, and Major Rogers retained sufficient consciousness to avail himself of this position; for whenever the elephant was on the point of kneeling, he managed to roll down two or three feet further on, so that the elephant missed his distance and had to rise again. This ruse was repeated several times, till they reached the bottom of the declivity, when Major Rogers could no longer roll, and death appeared inevitable. All hope seemed lost, and the elephant was just making a final preparation to squeeze the life out of his body, when the branch of a tree close at hand cracked, and the elephant thinking, I suppose, that it was some "human," rose to his legs, and scuttled off, leaving his victim, fractured and crushed, but still breathing, to be carried forty miles into Badula.

On another occasion, "it is related," (but, as an old Arabian author cautiously adds at the commencement of one of his most astounding facts, "God alone is all-knowing, as well as all-wise")—that Major Rogers having scaled a tree to escape an elephant, was caught by the foot by the enraged animal, and but that his boot came off, he must have been dragged down. The elephant's surprise at such an occurrence must have resembled that of the North American Indian, who seizing a be-wigged man by the hair to scalp him, found the whole *chevelure* left in his grasp. Although such escapes may occasionally occur, they are rare in the extreme, and even then, are scarcely matters of envy.

A very distressing accident, attended with fatal results, occurred on the Neilgherry Hills, immediately on my leaving Ceylon. A Captain W——, who, with excessive foolhardiness, had attacked an elephant alone, when unsupported by spare guns or other sportsmen, tripped and fell whilst retreating from one he had wounded, when just as he was rising, the animal hurried up, and with deliberation placed his foot upon him, and leaning his whole weight, crushed all semblance of humanity from him.

Our morning's march was rather a severe one. We halted at an old Brahmin or Buddhist temple, consisting of a cave scooped out of the soft rock, and ornamented with figures of many-headed and many-armed little gods, with spindle-shanks and unlimited corporations; there were also little wooden images of gods and inscriptions, and altogether it realized to the letter Shakspeare's description of

> "A hallow'd, gloomy cave, with moss o'ergrown,
> Where antique images by priests were kept,
> And wooden deities securely slept;
> The temple join'd of Nature's pumice-stone."

There was also a pyramidal, or rather obeliscal

collection of stones, of a considerable height. All collections of this nature in Ceylon are in the form of obelisks rather than of pyramids.

Shortly after leaving this sacred spot we came to a pass in the track that at first sight appeared perfectly impracticable, and brave indeed must have been the first horseman who attempted it. A mass of rock of the hardest granite projected in a shoulder, at an angle of 45° at least, right across the path, terminating in an abyss of 100 or 150 feet. To a foot traveller the transit was of course easy enough, though dangerous even for them if loaded, or without a stick; but for any quadruped, except a bear, a fox, or a chamois, it appeared utterly impracticable. D——, who had crossed it before, recommended our laying down wet comboys or horse-cloths, to afford some footing to the iron shoes; but one adventurous horsekeeper having accomplished the transit with C——'s excessively docile steed, we determined to trust to Providence and the horse's own good sense not to fall over. Punchy caused me and his horsekeeper a great deal of uneasiness; for we knew that if he gave way to any of his gambols nothing could save him; and I had the agreeable conviction that if anything happened to him I should have to be my own horse for many a long march; to our surprise, however, he crossed in the most careful gingerly manner, obeying his horsekeeper in every respect. I have seen some rather ticklish passes in Switzerland and South America, but I have never seen horses cross any that, to all appearance, was so dangerous, if not impassable, as this.

We camped, after a long day's journey, at a Cingalese village, prettily situated at the edge of the jungle, and shaded and adorned by groves of areca and taliput palms. The former is the most graceful of all the palm tribe. It attains the height of the cocoa-nut, some fifty or seventy feet, with a stem not one-fourth of its circumference; its excessive slightness and elasticity causes it to describe every imaginable segment and arc. It can even be bent to the ground, and this suppleness afforded the Cingalese kings a novel, and to them, I have no doubt, a very amusing kind of torture; it was not, by-the-bye, an entirely original idea, as Alexander the Great punished Bessus who slew Darius in the like manner; the amusement consisted in bending the tops of two trees together, and tying the leg of a criminal to each; the trees were then suddenly allowed to fly back, dividing the victim, and each taking its half of the "merry-thought." The areca-nut is gathered by children, who ascend these supple trees with ropes in the same manner as their full-grown parents do the cocoa-nuts. The taliput or palmyra palm, the very opposite in every respect to the areca, is even more wonderful in its nature and in its endless appliances. The eight hundred uses of the palmyra palm have been enumerated by eastern poets, but unfortunately, or rather fortunately for the reader, I have forgotten them. Its chief utility, however, is derived from its leaves, which in Ceylon are really used in everything, from tiling a roof to roofing a tile, from a house to a hat, and from a fan to an umbrella; they serve equally as tents, carpets, books, &c. &c. It is a squat palm, and grows slowly for many years, till, when some half century old, it suddenly springs up to a considerable height, and bursting with a loud report, spreads around numerous nuts, from which arise future trees. This unnatural effort on the part of the parent tree, like that of the queen ant or queen bee, is fatal; and the palm, like the fabled Phœnix-tree, dies immediately afterwards. The leaves attain a circumference of from thirty to forty feet, and possess a peculiar fibrous arrangement that allows of their being folded up like a fan without cracking. All the Palee books are written upon them.

The apathy and *insouciance* of these lowland Cingalese was this evening most remarkable and annoying. Our coolies were much fatigued with the day's work, and after pitching the camp, and lighting their camp fires, were considerably "used up." Scores of lazy, half-starved villagers were loafing about, and we tried to persuade them, with offers of money, and even powder and lead, to cut our grass, but in vain; no temptation of future benefit could overcome their dislike to present labour, however small.

Next day's march was tedious, but lay through some remarkably pretty country, and our camping place, by the rocky shore of a rapid mountain stream, was one of the most picturesque we had yet selected.

We reached Badula on the following day. Our route for a considerable distance lay through a grove of guava trees, the fruit of which, notwithstanding their immaturity and acidity, were devoured by the coolies in quantities that set one's teeth on edge, and gave one a *dolore di pancha* merely to witness.

Not being very anxious to gratify our followers' longings for an opportunity of spending their six weeks' savings in debauch and drunkenness at Badula, we passed through the town without halting; having, however, to overcome a certain amount of disinclination on the side of the coolies, by an equal amount of *striking* decision on ours. This evening was immortalized by the production by the Apoo of the very best curry we had any of us ever tasted. He was examined, cross-examined, and almost threatened with torture, to make him divulge the secret for our future benefit, but to no purpose. He maintained its excellence was accidental, and that he knew nothing whatever about it; the cook affirmed the same; so that I am deprived of realizing the fortune which would have been secured at one *coup* by selling this invaluable secret to the gourmands and gourmets of Europe.

Having a long ride before us to Newera Elia, we were up at cock-crow in the morning, trusting for the exact time of starting entirely to the regularity with which the gallinaceous males make in general their midnight and daylight calls. These "alectrometers," as they have been termed, keep remarkably good time, and their value is considerably enhanced by the reliable nature of their calls. According to the Arabs, who believe the language of birds, the cock says, "Commemorate God, ye negligent," but he says it in vain to the Cingalese, as they know none.

The forty miles' ride to Newera Elia was up hill the whole way, and very tedious: the last twelve miles were rendered even more agreeable by a tempest of wind, driving showers of rain right through you, in at one side and out at the other. Punchy, too, was especially annoying, and it required more endurance and patience than I possess not to lose temper with him. Every time I arranged my plaid, to try and ward off some portion of the deluge, he managed, by rearing, kicking, biting, and otherwise, to disarrange it.

Newera Elia was even more unprepossessing than when I had last seen it—the little stream was turbulent and almost impassable, and the rain was falling in torrents; all nature looked as if it had been draggled through a pond; the hotel looked green with continued rain; the beds and bedding were decidedly moist, the potatoes were like sponges, the cheroots you might have twisted round your fingers, and, to conclude, we ourselves were wet through and not very amiable. The only thing in the place to which you could not add water to its disadvantage was the brandy, which was of a peculiarly inferior quality, combining the worst characteristics of Betts's British and the foulest Marseilles Garanchine.

After such a moist night, not in an agreeable sense however, it was with the greatest pleasure we started next morning at daylight on our return to Kotmale. We had all contracted bad colds and bad tempers, and the monotonous torrent that fell unceasingly, and the dreary eighteen miles' walk through dripping jungle, did not put us in that beautiful state of mind with which every one is supposed to enter upon his matutinal meal. We breakfasted at the house of a coffee-planter who was in Kandy. The meal itself was an average jungle breakfast, consisting of young pig, jams, and various kinds and qualities of beer. After breakfast, we descended to the ford that had so unceremoniously stopped us at the outset of our expedition; it was now perfectly fordable, and we swam our horses over without any difficulty whatever.

About five o'clock, after withstanding the attacks of hundred of leeches of the most persevering breed, we reached the hospitable abode of our former host at Kootabooloo, and enjoyed the first comfortable bed and warm fire we had seen for some time. We remained up in that district some few days longer, during which we had the pain of hearing of cooly after coolie being taken sick with fever, till nearly every one of the thirty-seven who had accompanied us were thus suffering.

The coffee had progressed considerably since our departure, and the berry was almost ripe; its bright red colour alternating with the dark green leaves, presented a beautiful appearance. The coolies from the Malabar coast were fast coming in, and preparations for picking and pulping were being carried on with great activity. The crop promised to be a very good one, and I believe did not ultimately disappoint the planters. After a few days spent amongst hospitable friends in Kotmale, and some other districts, we returned to Kandy, thence to Colombo, and Point de Galle, where we said adieu to the "Mother of Elephants," and her hospitable planters and merchants. My companion proceeded, *via* Singapore, to the scene of present wealth in the Gold Regions of Australia, whilst I took ship for the land of past luxury and present lethargy, H. E. I. C. dominions.

THE END.